MENTOR OF MENTORS

LARRY THOMPSON

CONGRATULATION

50 YEARS

ANNIVERSARY

JOINED THE
NETWORK MARKETING
PROFESSION
MAY 4, 1968

"Larry Thompson: the man, the myth, the legend, changed my life forever!!! I became his #1 Student and one of the all-time highest earners in the network marketing profession in the world. Thank you, Larry. I will be eternally grateful."

Jeff Roberti
#1 Distributor Juice Plus

"The first meeting I ever attended in my life, I flew there on borrowed money and after watching Larry on stage I fell in love with MLM. Today, I have over 200,000 people that have changed their lives. Thank you, Larry."

Wally Kralik
Title here

"You can't really sum up LT in one word, but his HEART! To really know Larry Thompson is an incredible experience. He has been like a Dad to me."

Carla Angolio
Title Here

"LT, you were right. Thank you, thank you, thank you for your friendship, your years of dedication, your love for our profession, our industry, and for your lion heart! Congratulations on your 50 year Celebration as a true legend in our MLM profession. We love you and salute you, my friend. God bless all you have done. Long live Sir Lawrence Thompson!"

Jack Silva

"If Larry didn't have the guts to do what he did in 1968 we all might not be here, our industry might not be here!" - (man who talks about his 22 yr old daughter and the Kim/Robert event)

"Great things have happened. I have been able to learn from you, Larry, my biggest mentor in Network Marketing because of your training, your kindness, and you have always been there. So again, congratulations for 50 years in our industry! Motivating millions and probably this industry as a direct result has more millionaires that have been created because of what Mr. Lawrence Thompson has taught us. Again, thank you so much, Congratulations! Love you, brother! - (once a 19 year old scared shitless)

"We owe so much to you, Herbal Life owes so much to you Larry!" - (man who met LT December 1982)

"Over 30 years ago I met Larry Thompson. I want to thank you Larry, for what you bring to this entire industry and the many people you have affected in a positive way. We are really, really thankful for what you have done in this industry! Just keep it going brother, keep it rockin'!"

Jay Bennett

"I met Larry Thompson when I was 23. From that point on, my life was never the same. He saw more in us than we saw in ourselves. He has the magic!" - (name unknown)

The Millionaire Training

Golden Principles That Created
The Top Industry Leaders of Today

by Larry Thompson

MANIFEST
PUBLISHING

To order copies in quantities, call 972.632.6364.

ISBN--13: 978-1-944913-51-9

The Million Dollar Training with Larry Thompson

On February 21, 1981, Larry Thompson, the mastermind behind the Herbalife International success story, was recorded presenting the 1st official Herbalife International Training Seminar at the Bonaventure Hotel in Los Angeles, California, USA. At the time, Herbalife was doing less than a $1,000,000 a month. Four years later, it was producing more than $100,000,000 per month...

The Millionaire Training, a three-hour recording was a distillation of 15 years' worth of applied information, tactics, and psychology that Larry mastered from mentors and peers Bobby DePew and Jim Rohn who are considered the original strategists and personal development cornerstones of the Network Marketing Industry. Larry was very fortunate to learn directly from the source and to be able to share with you.

Keep in mind that there was no YouTube, Facebook, or any other training that an individual could access online like they can today that taught how to employ yourself, build a team, and essentially become successful.

The Millionaire Training has been, and still is, the ultimate full-immersion training for ambitious entrepreneurs, regardless of what company, products or services they represent.

There is no telling how many lives and companies it has positively affected since then. For perspective, *The Wall Street*

Journal called Larry the "The Original Architect of Wealth Building."

Today, Larry with his wife, Taylor, continue to teach these principles to hundreds of thousands around the world through their Wealth Building Academy.

Long-haired Hippie
Construction Worker

You want to know what this is all about? I'm going to share some ideas with you here that have helped many of us over the years (especially me), become successful. And, success is always relative to where you are and where you've been.

It's an exciting day for me. Since my first meeting at Herbalife and being involved with it, this is a training class that Mark Hughes (Herbalife co-founder) and I talked about since Day One. We're real excited about this – to be able to share some of the things with you, aside from our product line, aside from our marketing system, a very important part to make your business work.

I really appreciate those of you who have taken the time to be here who are not a part of Herbalife. You're certainly welcome to take some notes here today, and if this can benefit you and your business or your job or your profession or career, you're certainly welcome to some of these ideas. We're going to be talking about Herbalife primarily, and you should be able to use some of these concepts in all areas of your life.

You know, when I was sitting in the back of the room earlier, and I saw all the people out here and I could feel the excitement. Well, it made me a little humble to come up and share some of these things with you.

The things that I'm going to share with you today are things that are a part of my life. They're a part of me. They're not things that I developed. They're things that were shared with me about 13 years ago that made sense to me, and I applied some of these things to my life, and it started making a significant change in it. My background prior to network marketing was strictly construction work. That's all I'd ever known in my life. Construction work. That was it.

Back then, I lived in a small city up north near San Jose, California. Do you know where Livermore, California is? It's just a small city. I lived up there and went to school up there. I grew up doing construction work because my dad did construction work and my brothers did, and a couple of my cousins, and so we kind of had our own built-in crew there.

I started doing construction at 13 years old in the summers in between school, and I liked it. Quite honestly, I never thought about doing anything different than construction work. That's the only thing I ever thought about. It wasn't necessarily a goal or anything. It was just what I grew up with it. I was going to do it, and that's how it was going to be.

I do remember this, though. I remember my income goal. I did have an income goal back then. My goal was to earn $25,000.00 a year. Not a month, a year. That was 1968. I knew back then, and I said to myself, *if I can just get to $25,000.00 a year, I'm going to have it made.*

That's the only real goal as I understood it at that point.

Now it is springtime, and we're getting ready to go into our spring season, and I know what will be happening. I will be getting ready to come right out of the rainy season, like I had all the other previous years. It was around this time that I was fortunate enough to get exposed to a different kind of opportunity, and I never will forget that. I'd like to take a couple minutes here and share that with you.

It was my first exposure into the direct sales industry as we have here in Herbalife. A good friend of mine had found a little part-time business, and he got ahold of me one night to tell me about it.

His name was Mike Fuller. And, like me, Mike Fuller was also a construction worker. I really respected him because Mike was different than most of the construction workers I knew. He had a couple of homes, and he had a few dollars put aside, so I respected him besides liking him. I respected him a lot.

He called me one night. It was on a Monday night. I never will forget this. He was *very* excited (and Mike was not that kind of a person). He started telling me about this opportunity he'd found, and how he thought he could make some real serious money. He thought that it would fit me like a glove. Besides that, he sounded like he was walking three feet off the ground. That's how he sounded that night. And, he got my interest way up.

Even though he had gotten my interest up, I was hesitant. He had called me at 6:30 at night, and he wanted me to go over to the Hyatt House Hotel in San Jose and be there at 8:00 pm, which was a good 45 minutes away. I wasn't hesitant because of his excitement or because I didn't believe in him; I already knew I was going. I was hesitant because I didn't want to go to a meeting if my hair wasn't right. So, I said, "Well, you call me back in 10 minutes."

I was excited because of his excitement. And, I was curious about anything that could get Mike going like that. But, I had really long hair and a beard to match it. (I was looking pretty good, though! I got to share that with you!) And, so I did check in the mirror to see if my hair was right and if not, to see if I could get it going. I decided I looked okay and could go.

He called me back and I said, "Okay, I'm coming."

I was really excited about it. At first, I was nervous and everything, but I was excited because I'd never been to a business meeting before! I'm going over there and really jetting around because I have no idea what I'm going to see.

I'm more into the getting ready and what's going to take place than that opportunity he's talking about. Because it was a business meeting, I didn't know what to wear, so I just put on my best beads. Yes, I was that kind of guy!

I wanted to look the best I could. I went to the Hyatt House Hotel and I never will forget walking in. (By the way, I'd ever been in a hotel before. That's the truth! I'd been to a few motels before, but never a hotel. There is a difference.) My hair was down to the middle of my back, and you know, I was walking just right, doing everything I could to look my best. If you're going to go there, you might as well do it with style.

When I walked in there, I know the people thought they were hallucinating. That's the first time they'd ever seen anybody like me in there – a long-haired hippie. And, I won't ever forget it.

First of all, when I came into the room and sat down, everybody left. You know what I mean? Today, if somebody like me who looked so different walked in, nobody would think anything about it. Back then you didn't necessarily want to be the person sitting next to me, right?

And so, everybody moved away; that didn't bother me at all because I'm into everything that's happening around me. And I no sooner got there than the meeting started. The presenters got me excited that night. I never really thought that anything at all was going to develop from me going there. But they got me excited by some of the things they shared.

When it was all over, Mike's sponsor walked up to me and he looked at me and he said, "You don't want to do this, do you?" shaking his head no.

When I said, "Yes, I do," he didn't know if he wanted me to sign up or not. Well, I got started the next day. That first week, I had some incredible things happen to me. I got off to a good start because of Mike and his sponsor. Right away I got into a training class that was kind of like this, and they really got my attention.

In the first week, I earned $600.00 working part-time. I was just a babbling idiot after that, because I didn't think it was possible. I'd never made $600.00 working full-time in a week, let alone part-time. So, it was really something for me.

I remember what happened the end of that day. It was a Friday. It was five days after I signed up, and a gentleman who I used to work with came up to me to say hello. I wanted to recruit this guy. We used to work together doing cement work. So, I was drawing the marketing plan out in the cement there and telling about how you could do all this and you can do that, and he looked at me and said, "If it's so good, what are you doing here working in construction? Why aren't you doing this full-time?" I thought about it.

"By golly, you got a point!" And, I quit! I did! That impressed him. I got him into my business. And I left, I did. I left my tools and everything right there and I told them, "I'm not coming back." About two hours later I thought, *Hmmmm. What'd I do now?*

You get all excited and do all these crazy things. *What if $600.00 isn't going to come in next week? What's going to happen to my family?*
The most important thing that happened to me was that I got off to a really good start. I started thinking, *maybe this could really work out for me after all.*

After becoming full-time, the first couple months to 90 days were very positive for me. Then, I went through some transitions personally, and that's when these concepts that I'm going to share with you today came into play.

You see, when things are moving, when things are going well, you can do anything, and it'll work. But what happens when you stub your toe a little bit? What happens when you get a little confused? What happens then? When you're not sure of the direction you're going in. That's when concepts like this will come into play.

You Have to Drive a Cadillac

I was taking Mike's sponsor up north, driving across the San Mateo Bridge to get to the San Francisco Airport, and I had this black Ford.

Let me explain my car to you. I had this black '62 Ford, and it just wasn't normal – it was really low! I had lowered it to the ground so I'd be looking good driving down the road. However, there were a couple of problems with this car. Just a couple.

One problem was, it, didn't have an emergency brake, which was no big deal - only it didn't go into park either. So, when I stopped, I had a problem with it rolling backwards. I fixed that problem with a little cement rock I made, and I kept it behind the seat. When I stopped, if I was kind of going downhill, I just eased up on it, and put the rock on the ground so I could roll up on it. I got so good at it that nobody could tell that I was even doing it.

The second problem was it had burnt valves in it. So, it sounded like bloop, bloop, bloop all the time. Even though, I started making all this money and stuff, I was concerned. I didn't want to spend money because what if my success didn't last? What if it was a fluke? That was the truth of the matter.

I remember as I was taking Mike's sponsor across to the San Mateo Bridge, he looked at me and he said, "I don't want to ever ride in this dirty, blankity blank blank Ford again. Go buy yourself a Cadillac!"

He had a Cadillac, and he kept telling all his people, "You have to buy a Cadillac. If you're going to be in business, as soon as you start making the money, start showing the money here. Start showing people that you really believe in what you're doing. And that just didn't compute to me at all, but it was exciting!

I replied, "Okay, but listen, you don't understand. I can't afford a Cadillac yet."

He looked me square in the eyes and said, "Let me tell you something, Larry. You can't afford *not* to have a Cadillac."

"That makes sense to me!"

I came right back across the San Mateo Bridge. The Cadillac dealership used to be Buchanan Smith. Now, it's Lou Doty. I told myself, *I'm going to go get me a Cadillac* - never believing in a million years that it was going to happen.

First of all, when I pulled in the driveway, you have got to understand, I had my big, tall boots on and I had my hair down. I've got my beads and my little shades and, you know, they don't like to see me coming in in there, at all!

Of course, because my car is so low, it scrapes as I go across the driveway pulling into the dealership. I can see them through the window, and they're just having a ball with this whole deal. First thing is, I want to be as cool as I can be, and wouldn't you know it? I forgot to put the cement block down. My car starts taking off. I'm walking real slow and cool after it, until it started beating me. That was the first deal that happened.

The second deal that happened? I went inside, and nobody would wait on me. You know what I mean? NO ONE. I kept on walking around acting all cool. I kept waiting and nobody showed up – finally it was getting obvious. I'd been there for 15 minutes and I kept doing as much as I could to get some kind of attention to me.

Either they drew straws, or they got the rookie salesman to come out and wait on me. I'm not sure. They were all just having a ball with this deal, and finally this guy came out and says, "Can I help you?"

"Yeah. I want an El Dorado."

You would never believe how I said it. (I said it *real* good, *very* arrogantly. Mike's sponsor told me to be assertive and I was.) The salesman got very nervous because he could sense this was a real deal. So, he says, "Well, let me get my, let me get my manager."

Off he went to get his manager, and out came Gil Wilson. Now Gil Wilson and I have become real good friends since this, but Gil is the epitome of a Cadillac salesman. Black suit with the thin stripe, right? The little bitty, skinny tie. Black horn-rimmed glasses with the grey temples. Know what I'm talking about? That's Gil Wilson, a really nice guy.

Gil Wilson came out to me and he says, "Yes, can I help you out with something, here? What can I do for you?"

I told him what I told the other salesman, "Yeah. I want an El Dorado."

This was in 1968 and the El Dorados were very rare – they only came out in '67, and there were very few El Dorados around, maybe only three. I had to have something that was different, so I wanted an El Dorado.

He told me, "Well, we don't have any El Dorados available,"

I asked, "What about this green one?"

It was a forest green El Dorado with a kind of beige top, and I'm telling you, it was beautiful! It just really got me when I saw it, because when I drove up, the sun was shining on it, and it was just gorgeous.

"Oh, that one's sold."

"Well, what's it doing here if it's sold?" (I couldn't even believe I said that! I was really getting on with it that day. Feeling my oats!)

"The gentleman's supposed to come out and pick it up. He's supposed to come and pick it up on Monday."

Well this is Friday. So, I persist, "Well, I need an El Dorado. I need it today." Without missing a beat, I told him, "I've got a very important business meeting I have to go to tonight, and I need an El Dorado."

"I can't sell you that one today, but if he doesn't pick it up, you can have it on Monday."

"Monday will not work at all."

"Listen, come with me." He took me to the back where they were unloading the new cars off the truck. There was a gold El Dorado.

I don't know if you've seen the cars when they come off the trucks. They don't have hubcaps on them, and they're real ugly. They've got that stuff on them to protect them. It was a real ugly deal. I didn't like it at all.

I told him straight up, "I don't like that one."

"But you've either got to take this one, or you have got to wait until Monday."

"Okay. Let's go back and talk."

He took me back into his office, what I really call "the confession booth." You know what I'm talking about. When you go in there to buy something, you got to confess all your sins before they let you buy it. Gil wrote down a few figures on a piece of paper, and he slid it over to me.

I looked at it, and I said, "I'll take it!"

He couldn't believe it, right? Truth is, neither could I! You have no idea what I was going through there. I was having so much fun, and I had no idea what the end result was going to be. Then he said, "Okay. If that's acceptable to you, then we'll get the paperwork going."

"Okay! But, before we do the paperwork, I've got to be assured the car can be ready by 4:30 pm *today*. Can you get that car ready, because if you can't, well, I've got to know right now."

"Oh, I assure you, Mr. Thompson," (He calls me *Mister* Thompson now.) "We can have that car ready."

"Okay. Now, hold it. Can the papers be ready by 4:30? Because if not, I'm going down the road here to Smith Cadillac."

He looked at me and said, "I get your point." And, he started writing.

I went home.

I had about 45 minutes to kill. He was going to call me back to make sure everything was going to be taken care of, and I got cleared on the whole thing. Honestly, I never thought it was going to happen. I was surprised when he called me at 4:00 pm and said, "Mr. Thompson, come and get your car."

I let out a scream that you wouldn't even believe. I smoked it back to the dealership. I don't even remember how I got there. I do remember I drove my Ford right up in front, right there, and I left it; I didn't even try to hide the rock. I just got out and put the rock there.

When I looked up and saw the sun shining on my new Cadillac, it looks good! I can't even believe how good this thing looks. It looks much better than the green one, maybe because I knew it was going to be mine. I said, "Okay, let's get on with it. I got to get going on this thing."

I was nervous that I was going to change my mind, and I wanted to get out of there with my car. He told me, "Well, it's going to take about 45 minutes, there's one other client ahead of us here and my girl's working on the paperwork. It's going to take about another 45 minutes."

"I don't have 45 minutes! Can I just sign it and you fill out the paperwork and send me my copies?"

He said, "Well, of course I can."

"Okay. Let me do that."

I'm really going for this thing. I sign at the bottom knowing full well he can put any figures in there he wants! I thought to myself, *Well, that's all right. At least I'm going to have a Cadillac for 90 days!* You know what I mean? For 90 days I knew I was going to look really, really good!

So, I did that and now by this time (this is the truth) everybody in this whole agency is getting into this thing. The salesmen are into it, the mechanics keep coming out, some of them got their wives and a couple of girlfriends there, they can't believe this deal is going on!

We go out there and Gil Wilson is plenty excited about this whole thing now. He is really excited about it. He's explaining everything to me, how it works and everything, and I said, "Listen, I haven't got time for that, I've just got to get going."

"Well, listen," he told me, "in the glove box is the operator's manual. That explains everything to you."

Meanwhile, I'm pushing every button. I can't believe it. The seat goes every which way. I mean, this is just really unbelievable to me, this Cadillac is – well, until you experience something like that, you've never experienced it, you'll never understand that.

I'm pushing all the buttons and going back and forth, AM and FM radio, and I can even hear the dust on the needle on the station on my stereo – I'm convinced of that. And everything is perfect.

Finally, I said, "I have got to go." I started that baby up. It's backed in, and for those of you who live up north, you know it's a real long driveway out there. I adjusted the seat, got my mirror set on this one over here, got the mirror set over here, pulled the steering wheel down, brought it out, feels good. I said to myself, *This is it!*

As I started to leave, I told Gil, "Thank you very much, Mr. Wilson." Then, I buzzed up my power window and eased out of the parking lot.

Just as I turn, I'm doing two or three miles an hour, and I look up and there's Mr. Wilson kind of trotting alongside of me, and I thought, *Golly, what a friendly salesman, you know?* So, I gave it one of these deals where I kind of wave.

Then, I got that baby up to about 10 miles an hour and I can't believe it – I look up and there's Mr. Wilson, you know, still trotting alongside my El Dorado.

Finally, I look over, and see that I've got the boy's tie caught in the window! I slam on my brakes and he goes, "Oop!" with a friendly wave. I buzz down the window. Unbelievable. True story. True story.

If I can do it, you can do it.

About a year later, I was living out in Oklahoma, and I wanted to get another Cadillac. I called up Mr. Wilson and I was ready to tell him what I wanted and everything. The plan was to have my folks drive it out. I wasn't sure he was going to remember me at all when I called him. But, he certainly did!

I share this story with you for several reasons. Number one, I enjoy telling it, as you can tell, but also to give you an idea about where I've come from, what's happened to me, and what has taken place in my life. I think more importantly, to share with you that if I can do something like this and make the significant changes in my life that I've made, then you can, too.

It really doesn't make any difference about our ages, and it doesn't make any difference about our business background or education level. What makes a difference is about how we feel about ourselves and our opportunity.

I encourage you all to take really good notes as we go over this and hopefully it'll have the impact on you that it's had for a lot of us.

The One Variable is You

It is easier to make a lot of money and be successful than it is to make a living. It's difficult to make a living. Do you understand? It is not an easy factor making a living. It is an easier thing becoming successful, but it is not easier unless you know a few things. You've got to be aware of those few key factors that make a difference, and I'm going to go over them with you.

There are three parts to our direct sales business, and they are easy to master.

Of course, the products. I am not going to talk about the products. You need to master your products. You also need to master the second part of your business, the marketing.

Both of these are real simple.

Take an afternoon of two, three, or four hours and master the products and the marketing system, that's really simple. The third part of your business is the one that we are going to talk about today. This is the one that you need to work on and that's the YOU part. That is the only variable in any business.

If there's one person succeeding in your company with the products and there are 99 failing, then we know that the products are working.

If there is one person succeeding in your company with the marketing structure, and there are 99 failing, then we know that the marketing structure is working.

The variable is not the products or the marketing structure. The variable is the individual. That can only mean one thing...YOU are the only variable to your success.

What is the day of the month today? Is today the 21st of the month? There are people right here in this room who have already earned over $5,000 this month. There are also people in this room who have earned only $500 this month. Now, it's the same 21 days, it's the same product, and it's the same marketing system. Okay?

What causes one person to earn 10 times more money than another person? What causes that? It's not the product and it's not the marketing structure because those are identical. It's the person sitting in your seat, right?

It's not 10 times the contacts.

It's not 10 times the time.

It's not 10 times the experience.

That is not the factor. If that was the factor, I wouldn't be here today. Do you understand that? Because I didn't have any of those things when I started.

I didn't have them. It's within you. It's how you feel about the products. It's how you feel about the marketing structure, but most importantly it's about how you feel about your own personal financial future – it's about how you feel about you. I know that if I can do this, you can do this.

You got involved in your company because you were looking for something to change in your life. All of us have different reasons for becoming involved in our company, but we are all looking for something to change and improve.

Well, I'll give you a formula here, a real easy formula that I use that I personally got from Jim Rohn:

For things to change, you have got to change.

For things to get better, you have got to get better.

I'll tell you what the rest of this year is going to be like: exactly like the first part of this year unless you do something differently, and that is not only talking financially. Today's training can help you create enough self-value to start the positive changes in your life. It's about family, relationships, your spiritual life, your mental and physical health.

We're talking about in all areas of your life, not just money. If you don't like the way your personal life is going, I'll tell you what it's going to look like the rest of the year. It's going to look just like the first part of the year - it's going to.

If you don't like how your spiritual life is going, it's going to be just like it is.

If you don't like the way your family life is going, it's going to be just like this, okay? It's not going to change.

For things to get better, you've got to get better. For things to change you've got to change. It's a very simple formula.

Almost everybody I have ever met in my life, wants to have an above average income. Having an above average income is very simple: you've got to be willing to become an above average person. You've got to be willing to have an above average attitude, an above average handshake, an above average desire, an above average willingness, and above average excitement.

You become *above average* and you get an *above average* income. You've never met anybody with an above average income that isn't above average. See?

> You've got to be willing to become above average.
>
> You've got to be willing to *invest more time working on you* than on your job.
>
> You've got to be willing to *invest more time working on you* than on your products.

*You've got to be willing to invest more time
working on you than on your marketing.*

You've got to be willing to do that sort of thing because that's the real factor here. The first part we are going to do here is talk about the concepts of how to build up an organization. I will give you some notes on how to build an organization and I'm going to do a lot of abbreviating, but you'll get it down.

Now, how to build an organization? The same things apply on how to make a retail sale. The same things would apply no matter what you do. When you get the concepts down, they apply to everything.

The first thing is that if you're going to build an organization, you've got to know what type of people to look for, who to look for.

Dissatisfied People

Who do we want to look for? We have a lot of schoolteachers in Herbalife and a lot of people say, *Boy, I better go get me some schoolteachers*, right?

Well, we have a lot of doctors in Herbalife; let's go get some doctors.

We have a lot of professional people; let's go get some professional people.

We've got construction workers, accountants, we've got all types of people here. What type of people do I look for? What type of people am I'm going for?

I'm going to give you a common denominator that we all have here in the room and the common denominator that all of us have – it has nothing to do with our backgrounds at all. It has nothing to do with our experiences. There's one thing that we have in common in this room, and this is the type of person that you're looking for: We're looking for dissatisfied people.

Dissatisfied. See, it sounds a little strange, right? Dissatisfied. That's right! That's what, we've got in common. All of us in this room were dissatisfied with something.

We came to Herbalife hoping that Herbalife would change that for us, and I'm going to give you some categories here, and I encourage you to take note of these.

Financial Dissatisfaction

Of course, money, right?   Show me someone who is dissatisfied with their income, and I'll show you somebody that you need to be talking to, okay?

There's two parts to recruiting and you need to separate these two parts and that's what we do when we recruit, make no mistake about it.

We recruit. Don't you ever shy away from the word *recruit*. The most successful organizations in the world are the biggest recruiters in the world. Some of you in this room are familiar with the different colleges and universities and institutions out there, IBM, General Motors, Xerox; all the major corporations send their recruiters out to get the most talented people who can to go to work for their organizations, right?

That's what we do, also.

We send you out to get the most talented people you can find and one thing that we're looking for beside dissatisfaction in an individual - we're looking for one key factor also and that's called a *nice person.*

You ever notice that about Herbalife? You've got to be a nice person. If someone isn't a nice person, let's say they are really arrogant, they generally don't last long here because they just don't fit around our group of nice people.

There are a lot of nice people here, and it really matters to me when someone comes and looks at our business or our product line and when they leave, they say, I tell you one thing, those Herbalife people are nice people. That matters to me. I like them and that's the kind of feeling I want to have, and I know that's the kind of feeling you want and that's what we have.

Okay, two parts to it as we said earlier. One part is going out there and prospecting. Prospecting is the formal term in the industry. That's just finding somebody to talk to and that is all that is.

The second part is inviting them or what would that be called? Talking to them, right?

So, if you were going to sell a product, the first thing you would need to do is prospect; you would need to find someone to talk to about your products, right? Then you would need to do what? Talk to them. Two separate things.

So, we're looking for dissatisfied people and the first thing we've got to do is find somebody who we sense is dissatisfied, and then we're going to talk to them, okay?

But, what could they be dissatisfied with? How about income? I would say that initially, probably 60 or 70 percent of the people in our company come to look at Herbalife because of this, and we have an opportunity to make money here.

Doug Stunts stood up here and he told you, which is a fact, that he made more money last month than he earned in a whole year teaching school and that's a phenomenal success story, right? It's a very big one.

But when you take into consideration it's been less than a year that it's taken him to learn the talents to be able to do that, that is really phenomenal and that's the kind of thing that we need to pay attention to.

We don't have to accept things the way they are seen.

There's only been about a half a dozen things that I have ever learned in my life that have made the majority of the difference in my life. Not just from income, I'm talking about personally, a half a dozen things that made 80 percent of the difference.

See, the nice thing is you could have more than you have now. You can only have what you are, right? But you can have more than what you are now, because you can become more than what you are right now.

That's what's exciting. Don't ever let people tell you there is no opportunity left. There's plenty of opportunity. In 1950 there were 16,000 millionaires in this country. There are over 600,000 millionaires in this country today, right now, so don't you buy the "there is no opportunity" story. Don't you buy this "you better get something safe and secure" story.

You don't want to go for that story at all because that is all you're going to get. Go for opportunity and remember the 600,000 millionaires and all the millionaires that will be created this year. This is the first year (1981) that more than half of all the millionaires are going to be women.

There is going to be something for everybody here. When we are talking about income here, we don't need to be talking about those kinds of incomes. Listen, we started talking about making $5,000, $7,000, $15,000, $20,000 a month - you don't need to be talking about that kind of money.

Let me tell you what is exciting to most people: $300, $400 or $500 a month. If you would have shown me a way before I got started in the direct sales field, how I could have $300 left over at the end of the month free and clear, I would have been completely satisfied because I liked my job. I enjoyed the people I worked with. I was happy there.

The only thing that I wasn't pleased with was my income, and it never occurred to me that I could change it. You know that?

It never dawned on me that I could do something about it. I didn't know that I could. I thought that's the way it was because everybody I knew was that way. Everybody always had just enough money to get by. They did. I'm not making money out to be like it's everything because money is not everything – unless you don't have enough. You think about that for a minute.

What happens when you don't have enough? What does money become?

Everything.

Money becomes everything when you don't have enough. So, we need to face the facts here today. We need to tell ourselves the truth. What will get a lot of people excited? Three, four, or five hundred dollars a month.

When March is over, if you've got $400 left in your bank account to do with as you please, to buy clothes, to go out someplace, to go away on a trip, to spend on your home, to give to somebody, (whatever you want to do with it) free and clear, that would be something for the majority of the people in this country.

And now have another $400 left in your bank account at the end of April, and now have it at the end of May, and now have that at the end of June. You understand? That's a lot of money.

If a person has $100 free and clear at the end of each month, and now they go to $400 free and clear each month, it's not just an additional $300, they actually get to have 3X the lifestyle. That's a big difference! They have 3X the amount of entertainment they can experience. They have 3X the quality of vacation. They have 3X the quality of everything extra.

That's very important to understand – $300 or $400 is a lot of extra money per month. You do not need to be talking about "fortunes" to everybody. It's important to understand that just a few hundred dollars extra is a lot to most people. That doesn't mean that people aren't making large sums, because people are doing that.

If you show me someone who is dissatisfied with their income, that is someone that you need to put down and be talking to. So, dissatisfaction. Here is another area: Career.

Career Dissatisfaction

Their career is a life path that they are on, not necessarily by choice. It's what they've known. It's who they've been. What they are educated to do. And, now they are dissatisfied with it. They are not doing what they enjoy, or their company doesn't allow them the freedom and flexibility to enjoy their income. Maybe they've been a stay-at-home dad or mom, and now they want to get into a career. Where do they go? Where do they begin?

At Herbalife, we are an equal-opportunity career changer. Our top distributor in the company is Geri, she used to teach school and used to be a checker at Market Basket.

We don't have two marketing systems here, one for men and one for women. We don't say that if you are a man and when you become a supervisor you get 50%. But, if you are a woman you get 48%, do we?

We don't say that men have to do $4,000 in one month to move up, but women have to do $4,200. We don't have any of that, do we?

We don't say if you are a man on your royalty override bonus you get 5%, but if you are a woman you only get 4-1/2%. See? It's an equal deal here. It's equal compensation as equal does. We have a chance for a woman to step up here and create a career of her own if she wants to do that. I'll use my sister as a good example.

My sister, Tish Roshin, was looking for a career. My sister got started in Herbalife in December of last year with a kit. Her very first month, she took that kit and she earned $560 working part-time.

She was living in a brand new state, had only been there a few months. She didn't know anybody at all, but she got started. She was excited about the product because she lost 10 pounds on it, and she started telling people about the product. That made her $560 working part-time in December. And, she was loving her new career.

I'll tell you who doesn't believe it most of all. My sister doesn't believe it. She used to drive a truck. That's the truth. She was a truck driver! She's loving this whole thing. She's sitting back there. She's got a few hundred dollars in her pocket and she's looking really good, you know. She's doing really good. Now you know that a person can start right where they are and go wherever they want to go.

Let's talk about men. Put them in a separate category. Most men want a career. They get going out there and all of a sudden, they find themselves wanting something more or something different. I never would have gotten out of construction work if I hadn't learned of the opportunity from Mike Fuller.

I know I still would be there working construction and never know the difference, okay? I'd have been happy because I wouldn't have known the difference. I would be unhappy now knowing the difference, and being back there, but I wouldn't have been any less happy if I didn't know the difference.

But now that I know the difference, it's a world of difference. You understand? When you have choices, knowing things, becoming aware of things gives you more options for you to exercise.

I would love to get 50 men in a room with one thing in common: their age. I'd like them to be about 35 years old. I'd like to ask these 50 men one question, "So, gentlemen, you're now 35 years old. In another 30 years, you are going to be 65, and you're going to be retiring. My question to you is this: Do you want to be doing the same thing that you are doing now for another 30 years?"

If they were to answer us truthfully, what do you think the majority of them would say? They would say no.

And, if we followed them until they were 65, what do you think would happen? We'd find out that the majority of them were doing exactly what they were doing at age 35. Let me ask you this, "How come?"

Why would a person do something for 30 years that they don't want to do? Security? The answer is: They have little choice.

A 35-year-old man generally has a family and a lifestyle to a certain level, right? He does not want to take a chance and jeopardize what he has to start something brand new, even though he knows he wants another career. He tells himself, *Oh I won't be doing this until I'm 65*, but then 36, 37, and 38 rolls around with no change. Before he knows it, he is 62, 63, 64, 65 and he is doing the same thing he had no intention of doing.

But you see, he gets to 60, 61, 62 and you know what he says? "Well, it hasn't been the best job in the world, but I'll tell you right now it's certainly provided a lot of security for my family, good insurance, good retirement, right?"

You know what that's called? Justification.

He is justifying to himself and to his family why he did something for 30 years he didn't want to do. Now, I'm not putting that down. Do not misunderstand that at all. I'm saying he has got to justify because if he can't justify it, he's got to go to the local bridge and he's got to jump.

So, they've got to justify it, but I am also saying this: You take that man at 35 years old, and you give him an opportunity that he can work at his own pace. He doesn't have to jeopardize his job. He doesn't have to jeopardize his family. He can go at his own pace, his own rate. He can find his own space.

If he believes in what he is doing and believes in himself enough to try, I'm telling you, you better get out of his way because he will take advantage of it. So, when we are looking for dissatisfied people, I need you to understand the issue here, it's not just about money at all, not whatsoever.

Let's talk about another area here, it's called Challenge.

Challenge Dissatisfaction

Some people are just flat-out bored. Some people are making a decent income, some have got a decent career, but they are bored. Lack of challenge is a terrible deal to have. There's nothing that does it for the human spirit like the thrill of challenge.

When a person is challenged, they walk differently, they talk differently, they act differently, you get up in the morning differently.

Everything is different.

The way you talk to your lady, the way you talk to your man, the way you talk to your children, the way you talk to your employees and to your coworkers, it is different. Do you understand? When you've got a challenge in front of you, it doesn't make any difference if it's cold or it's rainy. It doesn't make any difference if it is hot. It doesn't make a difference if your tire blew out on the freeway. If you've got a challenge you've got something more important in front of you. You've got something more important than coming home and eating a little bit and turning on the television and going to sleep at 10:00 every night.

Sometimes it's money and career, but sometimes it's boredom or lack of fun.

Fun Dissatisfaction

Here's another one. This is important: This is called fun.

Show me someone who is dissatisfied with the fun in their life. Let me tell you, fun is really something. I mean, that – people enjoy fun right? I mean, fun is something. You can't even say the word fun without smiling. Try it. Say, *fun*. Am I right?

See? You kind of smiled when you said *fun*. You can't even get it out of your mouth without smiling, right? It doesn't happen. I mean everybody enjoys having fun. They do.

But we've all been in this situation before; we're sitting there and there's going to be a big party coming up in three weeks. And we are talking, and someone says, "I'm telling you in three weeks, we are going to have some fun!"

What happened to this time in between? I mean are we only reserved for fun in three weeks at this party? Is that the only time we can have fun? Or, can we have fun going to work and can we have fun taking rejection?

Can we have fun with disappointment?

See, can we do that deal? I mean listen, if fun is such a good deal, it seems like we should be able to capitalize on it as much as we can. Doesn't that make sense to you?

So, you know, the party deal, "In three weeks we're going to have fun," right?

In two weeks, "We're going to have fun at this party…"

One week, "Oh boy, one more week and we're going to have a ball!"

Saturday night comes around and guess what? It's a big bummer, right?

You can't just say okay, it's 8:00 pm on Saturday night, three weeks later now we are going to have some fun. It doesn't work that way, right?

Fun is either part of your life, or it's not a part of your life.

What causes people to not have fun? Lack of money. Lack of career. Lack of challenge. Boredom.

You've got these things going, and you're going to have fun no matter what happens to you. You are going to have fun because you now have the capacity for life. You've got the capacity to have fun. You can only have as much fun as you have the capacity to enjoy it, see?

You're only going to have as much fun as you are entitled to have according to your personal growth and your personal awareness. That is the only amount of fun that you can have.

So, you show me someone who is dissatisfied, and I will show you someone that you need to put down on your list. So, you get the idea of what we are looking for?

Identifying Dissatisfied People

If you are going to build an organization, you now know who to look for – dissatisfied people. Now, you can come up with a lot more categories than I've got here, can't you? I mean just go to work and write your list. Who is dissatisfied?

Now, if you find someone who is completely satisfied, you don't want to invite them at all, right? It would be a waste of your time. And when you find someone like that, do me a favor, take a picture of them and get a description so we can pass it around and say, "If you find one like this, don't invite them. They are completely satisfied."

I don't think you are going to find them too easily.

Okay, who to look for, now, we got that one done. We are going to put together a list of names of who? Dissatisfied people.

Let me give you some categories here. Let's break this list up into categories. If you are going to be developing up the organization, you are going to need a list to reference. If you are going to be developing customers, you are going to need a list. Here's the list.

How about friends? Make a list of the friends you have who you feel might be dissatisfied with one of these areas. The point here is not if they want to become part of your organization. The point here is not if they would like to be a supervisor consultant. The point is not if they want to be involved in the direct sales industry. That is not the point.

What is the point? If they are dissatisfied, they go on the list.

You say, *Well, I don't think they are going to want to do it because they don't have any time.*

That is not the point here, right? The point is if you feel like they are dissatisfied they go on the list.

Now, let's put another one down here. How about relatives? Okay, how many relatives do you have who you feel might be dissatisfied with one or more areas of their life? Write them down.

How about neighbors? How about coworkers? How about clubs, organizations? How about your church group? How about old high school friends, college friends?

How about anything? Just start to think here.

Friends, relatives, neighbors, coworkers.

I Shouldn't Make Money Off My Friends

Now, let me share something with you about friends. I have had people say, *I don't want to recruit my friends. I don't want to sell to my friends. I feel funny making money off my friends.*

How many of you have ever heard that statement, right? I've heard it. I've heard it a lot. However, rather than avoiding sharing this opportunity with your friends, you want to look at this from a different perspective.

Let's say you have a dress shop and one of your friends comes in to visit you. You haven't seen her for a while, and when she comes in, you're all excited and you're talking and catching up. You talk a little gossip and everything's going on getting everybody caught up again, and then she says, "I've got to buy a dress here. That's the real reason I came in."

She goes over and, on the hanger, she sees the perfect dress for her – the right color, the right cut, right collar, everything is right. She tries it on, and it takes five years off her age, she looks at the price tag, she can't believe it. She says, "I'll take it."

And you, as the owner of the shop say, "Hey listen, I wish you would go down the street and buy it at Bullocks."

"I'm confused," she says. "Why would I go down there and buy it? Is it less down there?"

"No, as a matter of fact, it probably costs a little more down there than you would pay here."

"Well, why would I go down there?"

You explain, "Well, Mary. I feel uncomfortable making money off my friends."

Now, if your friend has that dress shop and she has invested her time and energy and money into that dress shop, is she entitled to make a profit off anybody that walks in there and wants those goods?

The answer is, *yes.*

The only way you are entitled to make a profit is if you provide goods or services. It is immoral if you provide goods or services and don't make a profit from it. I'll tell you who expects you to make a profit on it, anybody and everybody who walks in your dress shop expects you to make a profit.

You are entitled to make a profit.

You need to get your thinking straight here.

You've got the finest quality products in the world to share with people. These are the finest quality products and you are hesitant to share them with your friends and relatives and neighbors and coworkers? If that is you, you need to evaluate you, not the products and the opportunity. You need to evaluate your thinking. Do you see that?

Get the point here where it belongs: if you are hesitant to talk to friends, relatives and coworkers about the opportunity, then you need to face the real issue here. You need to look at your thinking here and get it straight.

Now, it's not important if you still feel like that after you do it. The point is to do it any way you can. Do you understand? If you still say, "I don't want to talk to my friends, relatives or neighbors," then go talk to people you don't know yet, go put flyers out, run ads, do anything, talk to strangers on the street, knock people down, do anything you have to do. But you need to think about this one here. Get your list made. Does this make sense to you?

Get a list put together of 100 people. You might say, "I don't know 100 people."

Of course, you know 100 people! If you divide it into categories, you won't come up with 10 people if you think, *Well, I don't want to put John down because he doesn't have the experience for this*, and, *No, I don't want to put Uncle Joe. No, no, no, no. Not him, he doesn't have the time for this deal at all.* Right?

You see what I mean? If you start doing that, you can't come up with even 10 names. Your job here is not to think if it would be for them. Your job is not to think if they would like it. Your job is not to think if they wouldn't like it.

Your only job here is to think if
they are dissatisfied or not.

Remember there are two parts: **Finding someone to talk to.**

What's the second part? **Talking to them**! Your job is to talk to them. You think that they don't have the time? You don't know that. That's up to them! See what I'm saying?

Okay, now, we've got who to look for, dissatisfied people. We have put them on a list of names. Now, the next thing we get to do before we talk to anybody is, we've got to get our attitude straight.

Get A Gold Mine Attitude

Before you talk to anybody, you've got to get our attitude straight.

There are three areas to your attitude that you need to go to work on before you talk to anyone. We all go through periods of time when we need to do this, me included.

When you go to talk to somebody and you know your attitude is not quite the way you'd like it to be, don't talk to them. You're just not quite as positive, you're not quite this, you're not quite that, the answer is don't talk to them until you get your attitude straight. That's all.

This is simple. Don't go out there and deliberately set yourself up for a fall. Don't do that deal. Don't botch your delivery, there's no need calling him, he's not going to want to do it. You're right, save a phone call, right?

> ### We communicate with feelings,
> ### we don't communicate with words.

I used to be afraid of dogs. I really was. I am not afraid of dogs anymore. I got my fear of dogs down by going to a few training classes. That's true. Because animals communicate with feelings, not with words.

I want you to picture this. Picture a house that's set back off the street a little bit with a little picket fence about waist high with a long sidewalk like the old houses used to have, right? When you walk right up that little sidewalk, there's the front door. You have got to go in there, but on the gate the sign reads, Beware of Vicious Dog.

It doesn't say Beware of Dog. It doesn't say Beware of Bad Dog, it says *Vicious* Dog and you know, that's a whole different deal right there. It makes you look at it twice!

But you've got to go up and you say to yourself, *Okay, I'm going to do this.* And, as soon as you get there, that dog runs up and he's giving you his teeth and his snarls and he's gnarly. He's doing all that stuff. You say to yourself, *I have to go, I'm not afraid of you dog, oh what a nice pretty dog you are.* And, you start to go in there, and you're afraid of what's going to happen.

You know he's going to get you. He's going to get you, right? That's what's going to happen.

But as soon as you run back outside the fence, here comes this little four-year-old girl, she's never seen that dog before at all, and she decides she's going to walk up that same sidewalk as you do and as she walks up there, the dog licks her heels all the way up – the same vicious dog.

How come he doesn't growl and snarl at her? Because the dog can feel it, right? She's not a threat. The dog can sense it. So can people.

Have you ever talked to someone and no matter what they said, you just sensed that they were lying to you? That's communicating with feelings. If you sense something's not right (it doesn't have to be lying, it could be anything), you automatically don't trust it. You sense something's not quite right, because we communicate with feelings. That's the same thing that happens when you go to talk to people about your products, your business opportunity when you don't feel good about them.

You need to get your thinking straight first or they're going to pick it up, and that simply doesn't work. I had a lady come in once and she said, "I need some help."

I told her, "I'll do anything I can to help you."

"Well I can't get anybody at all to look at this opportunity."

I agreed, "You're absolutely right. What else can I help you with?"

"Oh, you didn't understand, I can't get anybody I talk to, to look at this…" blah-blah-blah and she went on and on and gave me the whole list of people she had talked to that day. Twenty-seven people and da-da-da and she said, "I can't get anybody to look at this opportunity."

"I agree with you," I told her, "Is there anything else I can help you with?"

"Are you making fun of me?"

"I'm not making fun of you at all," I said, "You just told me you couldn't get them to look. We don't have anything else to discuss about that, you're right. You can't get them to look at all. Can I help you with another project?"

As long as she's thinking that way, what is she doing when she picks up the phone? She's communicating it to them because just like the dog, she's going to show her products while thinking they're not going to want to buy. They're not going to buy, right? So, you see, she's right! This thing is not fallible, and I'm not telling you anything here that you don't already know.

There's going to be very few steps that I'm going to share with you that you don't already know. It might give you another viewpoint, but there's going to be very little you don't already know. Here's the attitude you've got to have before you talk to anyone about your opportunity.

You Need the Gold Mine Attitude

That's what you need, the gold mine attitude. I'm going to share a story with you here, and I want you to kind of go along with me on this story. Get into this story, and if I talk to you about the wind blowing, I want you to feel the wind blowing in your face. I tell you a perfect time for this story, Sunday morning. That's the best.

Sunday mornings are different, did you ever notice that Sundays have a different feeling than Mondays and Saturdays and Fridays? Sundays are different. Every day of the week has a different feel to it. Even if you didn't know what day of the week it is, you could almost tell what day it is by just seeing a few people and watching stuff.

Sundays are special, and I want you to think about waking up real early. I know we've all experienced this sometime, even if we don't like to wake up early, but I want you to think about waking up real early in the morning. Maybe 5:30 am. For some reason, you have no idea why you're awake. You look at your clock and see it's 5:30 am, and you can't believe this for a minute. But you feel so alive, so alert. Instantly, you're on just like that and you can't believe it.

The sun is shining outside, you can see it. You get dressed and you go out there and you start to make yourself some orange juice or something. Everyone in the house is asleep and it's real quiet, and you're kind of glad they're asleep because you're enjoying this so much.

You decide to walk outside and there's just that slight chill in the air, but it's going to be warm and you can tell it. The birds are chirping, you can hear them and there's hardly any traffic.

It's one of the clearest days that you've seen in a long, long time. And you're just enjoying it and you decide, *Heck, I'm going to go for a drive and head up to the mountains.* You get in your car and you start driving up into the mountains. You've got your arm out the window and wind's blowing, and it just feels so refreshing.

You get out to the foothills, you're driving around and finally all of a sudden, you start driving on one of your favorite roads, just a few houses on it. Driving around, you look up and there's a road off the right that you've seen before and you thought about taking before but never have. But, today you're going to do it and see where that road goes.

You start driving up this road and every now and then, you can catch a glimpse of the valley down below. And then, the road comes up here and you can see that there hasn't been anybody driving up here in years because there's no tracks. There is grass all over the road, and you get up on a little flat plateau there and you park your car.

You lean against your car, and you're looking at one of the most magnificent views that you've ever seen in your life and you can't believe that something this beautiful exists. As you're standing there enjoying it all, you look over to the right and there's something over there that's different, you're not quite sure what it is, but you decide to go investigate.

The closer you get to it, the more intriguing it becomes and if you get a few feet away, your suspicions are confirmed here. It looks like it's the mouth of a cave that's been covered up with brush. You quickly start pulling all the brush off and find it's a big cave and it goes for 10 feet and then turns to the right just a little bit, and the sun is shining right in on it.

It looks like it's a safe cave, so you decide to venture in, and you begin to get really nervous. As you are walking in, you have no idea what's to the right. As soon as you get there, you look to the right, and what do you think you see?

Gold coins from floor to ceiling! Wall-to-wall gold coins!

There is no telling how long they've been there. After you bite one and make sure it's real, next thing you do is look over your shoulder to make sure no one's following you, right?

For me, I'm going to get my car as close to the cave as I can, and I guarantee you when I go home it's going to be so loaded with gold coins it will be like my low riding Ford. If it is dark, the headlights would be shining up in trees, right? That baby is going to be loaded!

You get back home. Now, your wife or husband is awake and says, "Where have you been? It's 10:30 am, I've been worried. I've been worried to death about you."

You say, "Open the garage door quick!"

They get the garage door open and you pull the car in. "Where'd you get this?"

"I don't have time. Help me unload it," and they certainly do, right? You say, "Load that baby into the basement, I'll be back!"

This time, you go get a pickup truck and a U-Haul trailer. You're going to need a shovel, right? You stop by the local hardware store. You don't even go down to 'Pick and Save' to get it at 40% off. No, no… you go to the local hardware store and pay retail, right?

New shovel. And you get out there and you load that baby up and you still can't believe your good fortune! You go and unload that one.

You come back for a third load. But when you come back for your third load, something's not quite right. You're not sure what it is. So, when you leave, you take a stick and just put a mark on the ground. When you come back for your fourth load, you've got the answer. What you were thinking all along is true.

There's more gold now than when you started!

You discover every coin you take out, two coins comes in its place, and the first thing you do is get very excited. The second thing you do is realize you've got to have some help, right? Or, it's going to be out the mouth of the cave and the whole world's going to know about it.

So, who is the first person you want to help you? Are you going to run an ad? Are you going to go to the local unemployment office? Are you going to hang some fliers at the shopping center? What are you going to do?

Well, I'll tell you what I would want to do. I'm going to go get my brother, Johnny, right? I have to go over and get him. He has to help me load this gold up, right?

Now, I go over to Johnny and he's watching the Super Bowl. It's the last minute and a half of the first half. It's tied, and they're going for the score. Am I going to sit there and wait for it to get over? Or, am I going to turn the television off and say listen to this? What's more important, right?

You see, that's the gold mine attitude.

I know there's not a gold mine like that which exists in this country, but I'll tell you what, I would not trade what I've got in Herbalife for a gold mine like that. I wouldn't do it.

See Herbalife has got the vault door open and we're saying take all the gold you want. You can take it all. Everything you want. Come on in. You need some help? Get some helpers who can come and get it. Need some more? Get some more helpers. Get out and then get a couple more. Come and get all you want.

Just don't push, don't shove and don't be greedy.

The more gold that we take out, the more gold there is for everybody. There's more gold in the Herbalife vault now than there was a year ago, and the more people that come to the vault and take out the gold, the more gold there is for everybody else.

Now that's the attitude you need when you share this opportunity with people. You need the goldmine attitude. Okay?

And, here's a second thing you need to do. You need to get excited and enthusiastic, and if you've got a gold mine, you have no problem getting excited and enthusiastic – none whatsoever.

I'll tell you what, if you go over to your brother Johnny's house and said, "Come with me and dig the gold,"

And he replies, "No, I want to finish the game,"

Would you wait and say, "Please, oh please, oh please?" Would you think, *nobody wants to help me dig the gold. I'm going to go back home. Nobody wants to help. I'm finished.* Would you think that?

Are you going to call up wife and say, "Nobody wants to go with me. This is not for me."

If you said that, you know what she is going tell you. She is going to tell you, "Hit it!" right?

She is going to say, "Get somebody right now," or, "You stay here and I'll go get the gold!"

You see you have to be excited and enthusiastic about this whole thing. Now I'm talking about genuine excitement. I'm not talking about phony excitement. I'm talking about real, sincere excitement is what you've got to have.

You know you can come to one of these meetings and you'll get excited. You go to one of our meetings in any of our offices and you can't hardly even talk to a customer and not get excited. People can get you easily excited about this offer.

Things can get you excited, right? But I'm talking about real sincere, deep excitement that comes from within, and the only way I know to get that is with the facts.

That's the only way I know to get it. You've been at that gold mine. You've seen it and you've bitten into it. You've seen that every coin you take out, two more come back in, and if someone says, "I'm not going to go with you," you're not going to feel bad at all. You know better, and that's the same thing here.

People are going to spray rain on your parade. You bet your life they are. People are going to tell you you're crazy. People say, "Oh no, another one of those deals. Oh no, oh no." They're going to pull that deal on you. Makes no difference what they do. It only makes a difference what YOU do. I'm telling you right now, you can go out there and you can talk to people, and the most important thing is that it makes no difference if the people you talk to buy your story. What makes a difference is if you buy their story.

> It makes no difference if the people you talk to buy your story. What makes a difference is if you buy their story.

They're going to dump on you. They're going to tell you how bad your products are. They're going to tell you how bad your opportunity is. They're going to tell you how foolish you are.

They're entitled to say what they want to say. You're entitled to believe what you want to believe. Well the greatest stories of all, the greatest teacher of all, some 2,000 years ago had to develop His organization.

He had His, not Top 10, but His Top 12 that He spent three years training and teaching. And finally, the time came, you know what the story is, the time came for Him to send them out into the cities, and they were going to go out in the cities two-by-two. Remember the story?

And they were all excited. They were jazzed up. They were excited. They were going to go out and they were going to tell this story to everybody. They were going to convert the whole world over to their story.

The greatest teacher of all saw that there was something there and He said, "Before you go fellas, there's one thing I need to share with you. When you go out into those cities, not every home is going to be of your accord, and when you leave the home shake every grain of sand from your shoes."

Now, I thought about that one for a long time. What does it mean? *Shake every grain of sand from your shoes.* And I think I understand it. If you have a grain of sand in your shoe, one grain of sand won't necessarily hurt you unless it stays there over a prolonged period of time and it will start a little irritation.

As a matter of fact, you can probably leave one grain of sand in your shoe for some time and never shake it out. But if you've got two grains of sand in your shoe, now it's a little bit uncomfortable and you need to give it some attention, and if you leave it there it becomes increasingly more of a hindrance.

And if you get three grains of sand in your shoe and you don't do anything about it, the next thing you know you have a blister. And if you don't pay any attention to it then, the next thing you know, it's infected. The next thing you know, you have to have your foot amputated and it could kill you.

Is that the truth? From one grain of sand? Remember, it was important enough for Him to mention just before they left. And you know what that means to me? When you go out there, you think every person's going to be of your accord. They're not. And what that means is it makes no difference if they buy your story. What makes a difference is when you leave them that you don't buy any part of their story. And the reason you're not going to do that is because you've got the facts. You've got the facts.

So, your excitement and your enthusiasm are *genuine*. Genuine excitement. Genuine enthusiasm. Don't let anybody sell you their bill of goods at all. If you do, you deserve what you get.

Period! Over and out, you deserve it. If it's not genuine excitement and enthusiasm with sincerity, it'll get you.

As I said earlier, you can come to meetings and you can get excited. You can. You can do it. You can read a book and get excited. You can listen to a tape and get excited.

If there's one book that you can read in Los Angeles to teach you how to be excited, there's a thousand books you can read in Los Angeles that teach you how to be more excited and more enthusiastic.

If there's one course you can take for $25 or $2,500, there has to be a hundred courses you can take that would teach you how to be more excited and more enthusiastic. They teach you things you wouldn't believe. Actually, you would believe it because you've gone through them, too.

They teach you things like this: When you wake up in the morning, one of the first things you want to do is you want to yell as loud as you can, beat yourself on the chest and run to the bathroom. They claim you have to go anyway, so you might as well run, right?

Heck, I tried that. I got in there and felt foolish. I didn't have to go, you know. There are others that teach you that if you feel a little introverted to wear red underwear. That's right; they said you need to just wear red underwear. They think of it as the same concept as tying a string around your finger. If you need to get yourself worked up, just pull those babies out and look at them. Right? Oh yeah, more excited and more enthusiasm.

I tried that. That doesn't work either.

If you want to get excited and enthusiastic, don't wear any underwear and that'll get the adrenalin flowing right now, okay?

Look here. You know what this is here? Up and down, up and down. You know what that is? That's a new distributor's psyche.

That's what it is. New distributor's psyche. Up and down, up and down.

Let me tell you what happens to a new person when they come and look at our business. They get really excited when someone invites them down to see the opportunity, right? They get kind of excited down here when they come, and they see it.

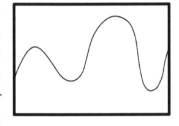

They really are thinking exactly like I was thinking over 13 years ago, *Well, you know, it's really not for me and you know, it's going to be for others, but not for me.*

Yet, they get there and they say, "Hey, this product sounds good." They start seeing a few of the people and say to themselves, *That guy's not any different from me*, or *She's not any different from me. Maybe I can do this thing.*

They say everybody's into health and nutrition. So, let's say it's a couple and they get all excited and they let you know they are going to start off with that senior consultant's merchandising pack. Let me start out right now. I'm going to go on this deal, okay?

And then, they get home and they're all excited and you're talking to them that night and they get home and the husband and wife is heading home and say to one another, "Hey, this is really something. We're going to go in on this. We should not be spending $285 but we can get it back; we'll use our vacation money. We got it, we're okay. Maybe this thing will work out well." And, they're all excited that night and they stay up a couple hours extra talking about it.

Next morning something real interesting happens – they both wake up before the alarm clock goes off and they're lying there perfectly still not talking to each other and not moving, looking straight up at the ceiling and they got this strange feeling inside their stomach. They don't know if they got the flu or they're in love again, right? You know the feeling.

And it's neither one; it's their $285, right? And they're scared. He doesn't want to say anything to her because he's afraid if he does, she's going to say, "I told you so."

She doesn't want to say anything to him because she's afraid if she does, he's going to say, "I told you so."

And, no one is saying anything but the next couple days the kids get yelled at a lot and the dog gets kicked, nothing's going smoothly there until finally, he comes home from work and he says, "Honey, it's Tuesday night and John's going to the meeting tonight. Let's go, it's going to be something." She perks up and they get ready. They're heading down to the meeting and they start talking now.

They went here, they were up here, down here and now they're up here, right? They're up here; that's where they are and he says, "You know something, honey. I didn't want to say anything about it; I've just been sick you know. I haven't been myself the last couple days because I started thinking what are we doing in this business? We don't know anything about sales; we don't have any experience. I'm thinking all I am is a plumber. I need to be doing this stuff here and the money we spent? I could have bought you new clothes, and I could have done a lot of things."

"But I'm telling you, I've got a good feeling about this Herbalife thing and John's excited about it too, – he said he thinks he could do something like this, and he knows a couple people who want to do it. I think we got something going; this is really something."

She says, "You know, I've been experiencing the same thing, and I feel good about Herbalife, too. I think this is something."

They go down there that night and start shaking hands and say, "Hi, my name is Bob, and this is my wife, Mary." They are going on and on introducing themselves to people.

Five minutes to 8:00, John hasn't shown up yet.

Two minutes to 8:00, and they're all looking like their dog just died...

Seven minutes *after* 8:00 and they're convinced that John is not coming and they slip out the back door, going home.

Whoa, way down here, right? And you know the conversation on the way home?

Bob says, "You know, maybe this business isn't for us after all. We don't have any sales experience, no business experience, and you know, if it was a different time of year, maybe it'd be better, maybe we made a mistake. Well let's try and get our money back anyway, okay?"

Things rock along for about a week and then all of a sudden, Bob talks to Frank. Frank says he's coming, he's going to meet them at his house next Thursday night and they're all going over together and he's really excited about this, alright?

So, here comes Frank, right on time and they get Frank down to the meeting – all three of them go down to the meeting together and they're all excited and Frank sees it and he says, "This is the best thing I've ever seen in my life! You can't miss with a product line like that and the people around here if they're willing to help you the way it all seems, this thing is, this is wonderful."

Frank says, "Listen, you can forget about building an organization, you can retire off of me alone!"

Got it? Whoa, way up here! They take Frank home and they go out for a drink, right? And here's the conversation, "We've been up and we've been down in this business, but I just feel so good about Herbalife; I know it's the best thing that's ever happened to us and maybe in another six months I'll be full time and the two of us can work together and we can do all the things we ever wanted; we can fix up the family room, we can get the new car and we can have this and this is so good; I'm just so excited about Herbalife!"

Frank backs out... WHOA! Then what? "You know it's the wrong time of year and we haven't had any experience in this before," right?

How many have experienced that? It's going to get you. This is what happens, okay? But let me point out something – do you think this is only reserved for new distributors, or do you think old distributors go through this?

You bet your life they do!

You think I go through this? Absolutely.

The difference is – if I invite somebody and they don't show, do I get disappointed? Yes. But not for two or three days – I'm disappointed for maybe two or three minutes. You just have to start hacking away at the time. This is not going to switch for you overnight. You have to hack away at it and instead of two or three days, it's going to be two and a half days and it's going to be one and a half days – you're going to start moving on it. You're not going to go from two days of disappointment to two minutes of disappointment – you've got to be a little bit better at it today than you were yesterday.

> You've got to be able to control your attitude
> just a little bit more today than you did yesterday.

> You've got to be a little bit more excited today
> than you were yesterday.

> You've got to be a little bit more sincere today
> than you were yesterday.

You've got to be a little bit more effective today than you were yesterday.

You don't go from here to here.

You do it a little bit at a time.

Never let a day go by that you stay the same, because I'm going to tell you something, you're either going up or you're going down – you don't stay the same and if you're not going up, check the gauge, it's heading down – you have no choice in this matter at all.

And the only way I know to control this is with the facts. That's how I keep my attitude up is with the facts. You've got to get excited and you've got to be enthusiastic, but sincere excitement through that only comes from the facts.

Here's something else you've got to have in your attitude – deadly serious.

You say, "Hold it, how am I going to be excited, enthusiastic and deadly serious at the same time?"

Here is a scale that we all fit on – up here's delirious excitement – down here's deadly serious. Everybody fits in there some place. Now if you're the type of personality that's always so enthusiastic about something, no one's going to want to look at your products or your opportunity because nothing can be that good, right?

If you're the type of personality that's so deadly serious, nobody's going to look at it either because it's too grim, right? You've got to blend in here. Of course, you want to – someone says you're excited about this, you don't have to tell them this, your attitude does – you bet your life I'm excited, but I'm serious about it, too.

"This is the finest opportunity I've ever seen." That's got to come across in your attitude. It does.

You'll see somebody come in here and they'll go right to the top right now. It's because they're able to handle that. They feel strong about the product, they feel strong about the marketing, they feel strong about themselves – it's not their talents – it really isn't – it's how they feel about it. Okay, does this make sense to you?

Deadly serious in your attitude. You bet your life you're deadly serious. You'd be deadly serious about any opportunity that you have. Don't be deadly serious about skating by – don't be deadly serious about Friday coming and it's a weekend.

You be deadly serious about your financial future and your personal future at all times and don't let anybody do anything that would detract you from that. Period. Especially if they're people close to you.

The people close to you are ones that get you – sometimes. They say, "Oh, I support you 100 percent in this business – anything you want to do is fine with me, I'm here to support you – go to it."

And then they'll turn right around and say, "Hey, why don't you come on over Saturday and help me out?"

You tell them, "Oh, I'm going to my business meeting."

They can't hold their tongue, "Oh, you're going to *another* meeting?"

That's called arrows of the tongue – *unintentional* – it doesn't mean they don't love you; it doesn't mean they don't care – but that's called arrows of the tongue, okay? It's sharp and it's piercing and after a while, you've got to understand the facts – that's the only thing that you're going to get by with here. You can't get to the top and be successful without the fact.

Death of a Salesman

What Can Hold You Back in Your Profession?

Let's talk about what is the *death of a salesman*? Or, we also can call this the death of someone in their own business, or we can call this the death of someone in their own profession.

There are certain things that hold people back, and we're going to talk about that. I will note this: no matter if you're in the sales profession, or if you're in the acting profession, or if you're a lawyer or a doctor or an Indian Chief, it really doesn't make any difference. There's one thing that is important here: We are all salesmen.

If we're going to be successful in life, we all have to learn to be salesmen. Let me rephrase that... we already know how to be salesmen. All of us do. However, the majority of us don't know it.

The best salesmen in the world are kids. Right? Have you ever noticed that? Have you ever seen a kid like that? Little five-year-old kid says, "Daddy, Daddy, can I have an ice cream?"

"Absolutely not. We're going to eat two hours,"

"Oh, Daddy, Daddy, can I have ice cream, please?" the kid goes on.

"Absolutely not. If you say that one more time, you're going to get it," the dad says just a little more tense this time.

Fifteen minutes later, the kid's licking on his ice cream, right? Kids know just how to take it so far, right, and get what they want. So, kids are the best ones.

Next to kids are women. Women are the best salesmen in the world. Uh, there's been very few things, ladies, that you've ever wanted from your man, but you haven't gotten unless you'd given up on it. Okay? Uh, that's really, really something.

The most important thing about sales is remember this: Salesman has an S in the middle. It means plural - more than one time, right? You can't just sell one time and now you have got the thing figured out and handled.

I'll relate this to relationships.

Men, you can't make one big sale to the lady of your dreams and expect that it's over. It's got to be every day that it has to take place. And ladies, the same thing goes for you, right? You don't make one big sale for your man and then it's all over, right? It's a continual situation, every single day. And you need to understand something about the salesmen profession, the most honorable profession in the world today. And, it is the most professional profession in the world today.

Everyone says, "Well, yeah, I'll tell you what the backbone to America is. It's the farmer, right?" Let the farmer stop producing food for 30 days. And, very little is going to happen.

So, you might say, "Well, the backbone is the legal industry." Let's shut down the legal system, the lawyers and the judges for 30 days. Again, nothing much happens. Let the medical professions shutdown for 30 days and nothing much happens.

A salesman stops selling for 30 days, and it stops everything. So, it is the most highly respected profession in the world. It's also the most highly paid profession in the world, too. It is salesmen, not doctors who make the most money. It's not lawyers, right? It's salesman who make more money than anybody else. And I'm talking about true salesmen, not someone that you walked down to the department store and they have a little badge that says, *salesperson*.

And, I'm just using the word *salesman* here. Ladies, please understand. Salesman is easier to say than salesperson, right? Just because someone has a tag here that says salesperson doesn't mean that they are a true sales professional. They might just be an order taker.

True professional salesmen are the highest paid individuals in the world and the highest paid in the sales field is in what industry? The direct sales industry. They make more money than anybody else in the world, so you've come to the right place for opportunity. You know you also come with the right credentials.

You know what you need to take advantage of this? Nothing.

You need desire and willingness. You need burning desire. It takes three things to succeed. I encourage you to write these down.

Burning Desire

It takes a burning desire to improve yourself financially. See, I don't care if a person is earning $500 a month or $5,000 a month. They could be a financial failure or a financial success either way. The key is, are they succeeding in their goals? Are they getting what they want for them and their family? Regardless if it is $500 or $5,000, isn't that the important thing?

Somebody says, "Oh yeah, I'm making real good money. The question is *compared to what?* Right? Don't compare it to someone earning less or more than you. You need to be comparing it to, *Are you succeeding in your goals for you and your family*? And, if not, the question has got to be asked, "Why not?"

It isn't because you don't have the experience and it isn't because you don't have the time. It's none of those things. The real issue is just you.

So, death of a salesman… When I'm talking about salesmen, we're going to talk about how important it is, and we're going to talk about what some killers are, and that you need to understand how important the sales profession is.

Sometimes we think badly of salespeople, right? Because you've gotten a lemon; you got stuck with something, so you blame the salesperson. But what you need to do is turn that around.

Think of any object that you have in your home that you like – your clothes, car stereo, bed, plants, anything that you have that means a lot to you. I want you to notice that you bought that from a salesperson. Understand? And you think well of them, you think of them as someone who's nice and a good salesperson makes you feel good about it because they continually sell you on it, and that's not negative.

I mean, they're telling you, what they're telling you is the truth, right? But they're continually making you feel good about it.

Here's what a salesman is:

A salesman is a mind maker-upper.

That's what a salesman is. A mind maker-upper. And because the mind fluctuates, the salesman has to do what? Continue to make it up, right? Remember I said in a relationship, you can't just make one big sale and you got it, because the mind fluctuates. If you want to know why relationships don't do what they want, it's because the mind fluctuates. You have to continually make the mind up here. You have to continually work on it. Okay?

Now, I'm going to talk about the death to the salesman. Death of someone being in business for themselves, deaths of any type of professional individual. I have to tell a story here. Maybe that'll help out.

We've all known somebody like this, maybe the guy at the gas station, right? He keeps the gas station going. He keeps everything going, all the customers happy. He keeps everything moving, everything going and uh, he's the best mechanic. He treats everybody nice and you say, "I don't understand why Bill does not go out there and get in business for himself. He is just so talented. He would do just wonderful for himself; he's made a fortune for his boss. Why doesn't Bill get into business for himself? We've all seen that.

Bill finally gets into business for himself. He lasts six months, goes bankrupt working in his own place. He ends up going back to his old job and while he's gone, his boss's business has gone down the tubes. Right? He's so glad to get back there now; he gets back there, and he fixes up his boss's business and it takes off like crazy, right?

We've all experienced something like that. Well, what happened? What's the difference here? Is it because Bill doesn't have the talent it takes? Bill has some things that he was lacking in his character that showed up when he was his own boss. It was to his advantage when he had a boss, but it was a detriment when he didn't have a boss, and I'm going to go over those with you, okay?

Let's talk about habits.

Habits

We all have habits. Everything we do is a habit. The way we talk is a habit. The way we walk is a habit. The way we relate to others is a habit. The way we eat is a habit. The way we drive is a habit. Everything we do is the result of a habit that we have.

Our success in life, or failure in life, or mediocrity in life is a result of our habits in life, not anything else. It's based on our habits. So, if we want to change that, then we need to go to work on our habits. That's the thing that we need to go to work on and zero in on.

A bad habit – you hear the thing that a bad habit is hard to break, right? We've all heard that but let me tell you what else is hard to break. A good habit.

A habit is a habit.

The fact that it's good or bad happens to be that it's relative to the individual in the situation, right? Bill had some habits that were good while he was working for someone else. But when he got into business for himself, he fell right on his face, a result of bad habits.

So, a habit is a habit, and the only way that you can do anything with a habit, the only way that you can change a habit is you got to replace it with another habit. That's all. You change it with another one. You have got to make that the predominant issue here, and then you can alter it.

I'm going to talk to you about a couple of habits here that will get you in trouble being in business for yourself. One is lying to yourself.

Even the most honest people in the world have a tendency to lie to themselves. You will tell yourself a lie.
Don't lie to yourself. Tell yourself the truth.

That is very easy to do when you get into this business. You find yourself doing well, then the next thing you do, you find yourself going full-time. You get out there full-time, and you do great here for about two months and then you start going downhill.

Takes about two months after being full-time for it to start catching up with you. I'll tell you what happens. You have only so much time when you're part-time to make it work, and you've got your momentum going and it's working for you and you say, "Okay, my income is up. I feel stable with this thing," and your decision to go full-time is accurate. And then, that momentum keeps carrying you for about another month or two months.

What happens in your business today is not a result of what you do today. It's a result of what you did yesterday. What happens in your business in the month of March has nothing to do with what you do in March. It has to do with what you did in February, right? And without noticing, you've changed a couple of habits in March and all your business keeps going up in production, keeps climbing, your income goes up, your sales go up because of what you did in February. You say, "I'm doing the right thing now because I changed this over here. And look what's happened."

But, it has nothing to do with what you're doing now in March, it's because of what you did over here in February. So, when a person gets in this business and goes full-time, their decision is accurate, but then they change a couple of things that they have been doing. And, it takes a couple months to figure out that what they have changed is not going to produce the kind of results they had in February.

And because their production keeps climbing, they think, *This is what I need to do.* And the next month it starts falling off and then they start doing footwork again. They don't know what to do. They start working on solving the wrong problem.

There's only one thing you need to do.

Basics

It's called *Back to Basics*. And write that down, *Basics*. You've got to do the basics. For those of you who are sports fans, you understand this. How many follow basketball very closely at all? I didn't use to follow basketball. But, I started to watch and now I know that basketball is very exciting, and I had no idea it was exciting at all until I got into it. I really, really like basketball now.

In basketball, because it is so fast, you can go along and just keep hitting points and everything is hitting it. Then, all of a sudden, you can go along, and the team can't make any points at all! It can be three minutes, four minutes, five minutes, and they put no points on the board.

Now, if they're scoring a lot of points, they know what to do. They keep doing the same thing, right? But what do you do when you're not scoring a lot of points? It's very simple. You go back to the basics.

You keep doing the basics over and over and over and over again. You stick to the basics. It's called the hot hand in basketball and sports.

So, all of a sudden, you're going along and you're scoring no points at all. Three, four or five minutes, no points in. All of a sudden, someone gets a hot hand. But, what do you do when you don't have a hot hand? Basics. Basics. Basics.

Keep doing the basics (and there's only a handful of basics here.) We're going to come down to it.

Now, one of them is lying to yourself. Don't lie to yourself. Lie to me. Lie to your sponsor, lie to your spouse. Lie to your neighbor, but don't lie to yourself. Tell yourself the truth. Have the ability to see it as it is and call it as it is.

You don't have to work a lot in this business. It's the easiest business I've ever seen in my life, okay? I've been in a lot of businesses and made a lot of money in a lot of businesses, but I'd say I've never done anything like this. This is the easiest thing I've ever done in my life! Maybe I shouldn't be telling you that. I'm hesitant to say that, but it is easy.

When my sister can start and 90 days later, have a royalty check of $2.010.88 her third month, that's unheard of, okay? That is unheard of, so it's an easy business to do, but don't lie to yourself about what you're doing.

Tell yourself the truth. All you need is eight hours a day, five days a week, every single week for three months straight, and you'll never have to worry about your financial future again.

When I first went full-time, I was told, "All you have to do, Larry, is work half as hard here, as you did in construction work and you'll be wealthy quick." And I said, let me at it. Half as hard? I'll work twice as hard, right? It didn't work that way at all because of habits. Understand? Habits.

One of them is lying to yourself... "Oh, I know what's coming! I got it going now, I've got it coming in now," right? Well, where is it? It is the only thing you have to ask yourself , "Where's the production today?"

Some people get so engrossed putting projects together, brochures together, big schemes, booklets, everything else together, that they don't produce today! They don't make one sale today. They don't recruit one person today. They don't really seriously talk to anybody about the product or the opportunity today.

I'll tell you how to make $5,000 a month in his business. I'll tell you how to do it and it'll take 90 days, if you will do two things:

Number one: Sell the product at every opportune moment.

That doesn't mean that you go out here and go door-to-door. It doesn't mean you get party plans. It doesn't mean you have to go to office buildings. It doesn't mean that. Sell the product at every opportune moment. Wear your button (Lose Weight Now, Ask Me How), open your ears, open your eyes, pay attention, and sell the product at every opportune moment.

Number two: Sponsor 10 people a month.

I've told this to some of you before, and I'll tell you this again, "There's not a person that's heard this before, who did it, who is making less than $5,000 a month. Period, over and out. That's what I told my sister to do, and that's exactly what she's doing. That's something. That's all she's doing is those two things. Sell the product at every opportune moment and sponsor 10 people a month.

That doesn't mean 11 in March, nine in April! Sponsor 10 people every month. And sell the product at every opportune moment. You can do that and $5,000 a month is yours. It's waiting for you, but don't lie to yourself here. OK?

Who did you talk to TODAY about the product? Who did you talk to TODAY about the opportunity? Don't tell me about what's going to happen next week with all these big plans you have. Don't you do that! What did you do TODAY that made a significant difference in your financial future? What was it TODAY?

You are the only one that's got to have the answer to that question, but tell yourself the truth on it, okay?

I'm going to give you a problem here, but I'm going to give you a solution to it. Procrastination.

Procrastination. I don't know how to spell it. I was going to look it up this morning, but I thought I'd do it on Monday.

I just want to see if you're awake. Okay, procrastination. How many of you are procrastinators? All of us have procrastinated. All of us. There's not a person in the world who is not a procrastinator in some area. Procrastination.

Procrastination took me awhile to understand and I had to relate it, but there were a couple of things that really got to me. I didn't think I was going to be able to make it. Even though I was making money and stuff, it wasn't secure money to me. See, it wasn't any of that stuff because I didn't think that I was going to be able to get it put together. And procrastination was one part of it, and it took construction work to get me back to understanding procrastination.

I couldn't understand it. Some things I just keep putting off and off and off and off, and other things I'd do right now, and I just didn't have any handle on why I did that. I didn't understand it. Let me share a story with you about procrastination.

The Fried Bologna Sandwich

We're in the nutritional business, but I'm going to tell you right now my favorite sandwich in the whole world, and I love sandwiches. I mean I don't just like sandwiches, I love them, just love them. And my favorite sandwich in the whole world is a fried bologna sandwich. Any of you ever had a fried bologna sandwich? Let me tell you - you never had one in the world like I can make it. Sometimes I will prepare a fried bologna sandwich, and you'll never believe it. You'll never be the same again in your life over this.

When I did construction work, you know what I had every day for lunch? Fried bologna sandwich. It's got to be prepared, right? It's got to be eaten, right? It's so good. You have no idea. And I'd been in sales about a year, and I was having tough times. I was making money and everything, but I was having some rough times because I wasn't secure as I said. I was nervous about it all the time.

It was a day that I planned to be off. It was in March and I wanted to do some work on my deck. I was building a deck out there and I've been piddling around with it and I was going to take a day and really get on with it. I was there by myself and I never will forget it. I didn't want to eat anything in the morning at all, because I don't like to get all bogged down. And I had it figured out where I could do X amount of work and stop about 1:00, rest a little bit, and prepare a fried bologna sandwich and eat it leisurely at 2:00. It was going to be so good.

And I kept working, right? Finally, I got down and it was time to eat my fried bologna sandwich. I prepared it and all of a sudden,

I'm eating this fried bologna sandwich. (And it had been a while since I'd had one because I hadn't been doing construction work for some time.) And for some reason, this fried bologna sandwich didn't taste nearly as good to me is I felt like it should, and that was bothering me.

I'd trained myself enough by now to pay attention to things that didn't feel quite right; to analyze them and figure it out and change it. And for whatever reason, I couldn't figure it out. And then it got me. I understood it. You know what it was? I don't like the crust. Terrible, right? I don't like eating the crust, but you also can't throw the crust away because there are starving kids in India, right? (You know how your Mother put you through that deal, right?)

So, you can't throw the crust away. And so, what do you do? I looked at the sandwich. I started over here in this corner and I started eating in the middle and it was ending up that I was going to have this big piece of crust left at the end. You know, it's dry, it's terrible tasting; nothing good about that deal at all, and then it hit me.

I figured it out, and I related that to *procrastination*. I said to myself, *I know how to do it now - make the whole sandwich taste good from start to finish.* You know what you do?

Eat the crust first. You get on with the crust! You eat little pieces of the crust at a time until it's all gone. You don't mind eating the crust because you know you'll get down to the last bite, which is the heart, right? The good stuff is in the heart of the sandwich. Everything is there, in the maximum! Whatever you have on your sandwich, it's all in the middle of the good stuff, right? And that's the best bite, right?

So, you save that for last. So, the point on procrastination is, all of us procrastinate in some areas of our life, right? We procrastinate when we're doing things we don't like to do. We hurry up and do this stuff that we like to do, and we prolong the stuff we don't like to do. And, why we're doing the things we like to do like eating a bologna sandwich, we're thinking of the crust, and we're not enjoying this to full capacity, right?

So, if you eat the crust first, the crust is more palatable because you've got all the good stuff to look forward to.

So, all that means is that the things that you don't like to do, you do first. And while you're doing them, they're more enjoyable because you're looking forward to the things that you do like to do, okay?

> **Do the things that you don't like to do first. And while you're doing them, they're more enjoyable because you're looking forward to the things that you do like to do.**

Does that make sense to you? All of us procrastinate, all of us do, but the thing on procrastination is, do the things you don't like to do first so you can look forward to doing the things you enjoy doing, okay? Now here's the next point.

Failure to Set Good Goals and Plans

Now everybody that you've ever met who is successful has always said you've got to have goals and plans. Well, that's one thing that almost hung me up because I didn't think I had them. I attended seminars, and they call it, *The Art of Setting Goals*. Can you believe that? I'd been to a six-hour seminar, *The Art of Setting Goals*.

Well I thought I couldn't master setting goals, right? They told me to write it down on the three by five card. Put it in your pocket, read it in the morning and as soon as you get up, read it at night before you go to bed. They teach all that stuff, right?

I'm not saying don't do that, I'm saying do that. For me, when I wrote it down, nothing happened. I read it, nothing happened. I don't know how to make plans. I don't know how to follow up. I didn't want to do that.

I was making money. I was moving ahead, but it wasn't with ease, you understand? It wasn't secure movement forward, and then I realized something, and that made a lot of difference to me; and what I realized was I do know how to set goals.

You know why? Well I had some goals in my life. I didn't write them down. All of us in this room know how to set goals. All of us right now know how to make plans to achieve those goals, and right now you don't have to read any books.

You don't have to go to any seminars, you don't have to do anything. You know right now how to do it.

A goal is something that you have got to have - you have to have it. If you have got to have it, and you become aware of it, then you'll figure out the plans. The plans will come to you.

I'm going to tell you a story. When I tell you this story, I bet there's a lot of people in this room that could tell me a story just about like that. There's only a couple of things early on in my life that I knew I wanted. One of them was my own home. I knew at the age of 13, I wanted to own my own home.

And, I was very aware I was going to own my own home. When I was 19, I was doing construction work on a track of homes and they had this one model over there that I really liked. I just kept going back and looking at it, going back and walking through it. It wasn't that it was the best model, but it was the only one that I could identify with possibly being able to get, right? That alone made it the best for me - and I just kept going back and looking at it and finally the developer said, "Why don't you buy it?"

"Oh, you know, I don't have any money or anything and I don't have any credit and all this stuff," I went through the whole thing.

"Listen, why don't you just go buy it?" And he said, "I'll help you. You can do some extra stuff and work off some of the down payment."

"Well I don't know."

He looked at me squarely, "Do it," and he walked off.

So, the next day on Sunday, I went into the sales office and I wrote out a check for a $250 deposit to hold the house. And, I signed the papers knowing the whole deal was a real deal because if I didn't do it, my money is gone right? So, $250 is a lot of money, especially back then, a lot of money. The house was going to be completed in six months. I had no idea where I was going to get the money for the down payment. The truth of the matter was I had no idea how was going to come in and cover the $250 check! That's true.

But I somehow knew that check was going to get covered before it got into the bank the next day. I knew that somewhere it was going to happen. Somebody was going to buy something I had, you know, my old tennis shoes, something! Somebody was going to give me that $250.

When I signed the papers on the house, I had no idea about how I was going to pay for the payment, had no idea how I was going to qualify, but I forgot all about that once I made the commitment.

I went out there when they started to level off the lot for the foundation. I took pictures, talked to the guys. I went out there when they were doing the foundation. When I did the cement work, I had all my friends over, and we put up some really special cement work. It was just really something. I was really excited about it.

And when they started putting up the walls and everything, I'd bring over all my friends and I would explain to them how the family room was going to be, and how the master bedroom would be, and how we would have the sliding glass door look out over the backyard. It was going to be a step down and I went through that whole deal.

They put the fireplace up, and I went out there and showed them how the fireplace was going to work and everything.

I had no idea how I was going to get the money, but you know the story. Almost to the day and the hour that it came for the final payment for the down payment to get in there. You know what happened? I had the money. Now, I didn't sit down and write it down on a piece of paper. I didn't do that. I didn't read it three times a day, two times a day like they teach it, and I'm not saying that's bad.

I'm saying it was just a total part of my awareness.

Now that story might sound unusual to you, but how many times have you had something like that happen to you?

That's a goal.

You know how to set goals and you know how to make plans.

You know how to do it today.

The difference between $10,000 a year income and $10,000 a month income is the *got to*. That's all. It only has to do with your desire, something that you've got to have. There's never been a goal in your life that you've had that you've not achieved unless you've given up on it.

Have you ever been in a situation where if, *I don't get another $200 the whole world is going to collapse,* and sure enough you got it, right? Because you had to have it.

The difference between $200 and $200,000 is not the issue.
The amount is not the issue. The issue is the desire, the amount of desire that you have.

I'm telling you the reason that most people don't make $10,000 a month is they don't have the desire to make $10,000 a month - they don't have to do it.

Now, if you've got to have a $10,000 a month income, as bad as you have to have the house, or as bad as you have to have that new suit, or as bad as you have to have that vacation for your lady, or as bad as anything you've ever wanted that you weren't going to give up on... I'm telling you, it's yours. It's a matter of time. It belongs to you. Just a matter of time.

How to Employ Yourself

Now, I'm going to share one other thing with you that will bring this together for you as far as, how do we put all this into practice every single day? How do we go from 8 o'clock this morning to 5 o'clock this afternoon? How are we going to do it?

It's a subject that I call, *employ yourself.*

Why don't you get out a fresh piece of paper for this? Employ yourself. Habits, remember the habits thing? The only way you can get rid of a bad habit is to replace it with a good habit, right? And you've just got to keep switching it. I'm going to talk to about employing yourself, how to employ you.

Everyone says, "It's okay to talk to yourself, but don't answer," right? Don't you buy that story. You want to really get excited. You want to have a good conversation with yourself:

"Yeah, but let me tell you this."

"Yeah, but what about this," right?

And then, just slap yourself around.

You've got to do it sometimes. You've got to get intense just like there was somebody else there. You've got to talk with the inflections, the whole deal. You can't say, "Well, the reason you're not doing well, Larry..." that just doesn't cut it. I had to learn how to employ myself. Sometimes, we need crutches to get us through life. Sometimes, we need mental crutches to get us through life, mental crutches.

You're up here on this stage, and you fall down and break your ankle. You're all by yourself. There's not one other person in this hotel. You fall down right here and break your ankle. You've got to

66

get off the stage, down the aisle, down the corridor, past the coffee shop, out the front door, across the street to the parking lot to get to your car. You've got a broken ankle.

Can you get there? Yeah. Would it be painful? Absolutely. And if you're all by yourself, there's not one person to help you. You could get there, absolutely you can. It'd take a long time, and you could do some irreparable damage to your ankle, right?

You're up here, all by yourself. You fall down and break your ankle, but perhaps you can find something that you can use as a *crutch*. And now, you go down the corridor, across the parking lot, and out to your car.

Can you get there? Can you get there easier? Can you get there with less pain? Probably zero damage to your ankle, right?

So, if you have the ability to have a crutch, then you need to use it.

Sometimes we need mental crutches to make us successful.

Mental crutches. And, that's what I had to develop was a mental crutch. I had to play mental tricks on myself. And to do that, I had to split my personality into two people.

I had to have two personalities, *Larry One*, and *Larry Two*, okay?

Larry One was the boss.

Larry Two was the employee.

Now, I had to split my personality, and I had to talk to myself, and I had to rationalize this whole thing. You want to picture it like this. What if you found out that somebody had a position, or better yet, you just met someone, and you got to like them. They got to like you, and you had no idea what kind of business they were in, but you just liked each other a lot.

And then, after a day or so there, he says, "Hey, listen, I really like you, and I think you're the type of person I'm looking for in my new company, and I've got a position for the right person. It pays $100,000 a year."

And quickly, he's got your attention, right? And you think, *Yeah, I know, it couldn't be me.* Right? And he says, "And I think you're the person for the job." Now, if that happens, someone would have your attention. What happens when you go out to find a job, for example?

You come in contact with somebody, if it's by virtue of an advertisement, personnel agencies, whatever it might be, when it finally gets down to where there is the basic company you would like to work for, and you're the basic person they'd like to have, then you start talking about income. Then you start talking about fringe benefits. Then you start talking about days that you work, hours that you work, etc.

Isn't that how it works?

Well, that's the same thing it is when you go to work for yourself.

The only difference is you don't have this person here that's overseeing you. Remember the bad habits? Remember the guy at the gas station here? We talked about him earlier, why he fell down. Because he kept some prior bad habits that were bad for his business, right?

He showed up when he was working for someone else, but he didn't show up when he was working for himself. Larry One here, and Larry Two.

Larry One says, "Hey, I've talked to you enough for the last two days. I've got something that I think would fit you. It'd pay you $100,000 a year." Larry Two is excited, "Tell me all about it."

Larry One explains his opportunity to him. And Larry Two says, "Okay, what do I have to do exactly?"

"I need you to talk to 10 people a day, okay?

"No problem. I can talk to 20 people a day for $100,000 a year."

"Hey," Larry One says, "only 10."

"All right, when do you want me to start?"

"Right away. How about starting on Monday morning, okay?"

Larry Two is chopping at the bit, "Okay, I'll start Monday morning."

"Okay, we've already decided for this $100,000 that you're going to work six days a week. Is that correct?" Larry One asked.

"Yes."

"We also decided that you're going to work at least eight hours a day during that time period. Is that right?"

Larry Two assured him again, "Yes."

"And you're going to talk to 10 people a day? That's the most important thing that I want," Larry One confirmed.

"I got it."

So, Larry One asks, "Okay, what six days a week do you want to work?"

Larry Two says, "Oh, I don't care," right? (Well, he's got to care, as to his future. You ever see someone go into a restaurant, and they say, "What do you want to order?" and they reply, "Oh, I don't care. Get me anything." Well, you know what you get? Anything. It's what you get. You don't get what you want. You get whatever someone else brings you. You need to care about what happens to you in your life.

So, Larry Two says, "All right, I want to have Sundays off."

"Fine. So, you're going to work eight hours a day?"

"Yes."

"What hours do you want to work, Larry Two?"

Larry Two replies, "Well, I don't care," right?

Larry One digs in, "Well, you choose it."

Larry Two, huffs, "So, okay, I'll start a 9:00. Say 9:00 to 5:00."

Larry One shakes his hand, "You got it!" Okay?

So, everything's all set. Larry Two's excited. He can't wait for Monday morning to come around, start his new job, his new career, making $100,000 a year. All he's got to do is talk to 10 people a day. He's got this in the bag. He can't even believe it. He's not going to believe it until he gets his first check, not ever. He's all excited.

Now, Monday morning rolls around, and Larry Two's ready to go to work. He's trying to get out the door to go do his job. He agreed to start to work at 9 o'clock, and just before he gets out the door, something happens with the kids and with the dog, and he gets a phone call. And as he's heading out the door, it's not 9 o'clock. It's 9:07 when he looks at his watch.

He thinks to himself, *It's 9:07… Oh that's all right. I'll make up for it.* And he goes to get in his car and starts it up, and he looks in his rearview mirror, and who do you think is sitting in the back seat? Larry One.

And Larry One says, "I could be mistaken here, Larry Two, but my watch says 9:07."

Larry Two instantly says, "Oh, you're right. It is 9:07, and I said I was going to start at 9:00, but a lot of things happened," and proceeds to tell Larry One the story.

And Larry One says, "Hold it, right now. You and I agreed that you were going to start at 9 o'clock, and the first day on the job, it's 9:07. Now, if you want to start at 9:07, Larry Two, that's fine with me. But you're going to start at 9:07 every day. It's not going to be 9:08 or 9:17. Whatever time you say you're going to start; you're going to start. Now, do I make myself clear?"

Now, if Larry One didn't care about Larry Two, what would he do?

He'd say, "That's okay. You make up for it a little bit later," right? Isn't that what he'd do? And what does Larry Two develop the first day on his job? *A bad habit.* Larry One cares about Larry Two, so he's not going to allow this bad habit to creep in.

Your habits are what equals your income.

The habits that you have is equal to your income, good, bad or indifferent. And for things to change, what's the formula? You've got to change. You understand? For things to change, you've got to change. So, you've got to change the habits. That's all it is, the habits.

Everything goes along well for a couple weeks when Larry Two is starting to leave, he gets a phone call from one of his best friends that he hasn't seen in six years, and his friend says, "I'm just around the corner. I'm coming over to see you."

And he says, "I'll be here." And he gets there, and they get to talking, and they get all caught up in all those war stories, all the things that's gone on in their lives.

They're going on and on and on, and before you know it, it's 7 or 8 o'clock at night, and he hasn't even gone to work at all. Period. And Larry Two convinces himself, *That's okay. I've got Bob here. Bob is going to be better than any 10 people I could talk to today. This is going to be something. I know he's just going to do great, and he'll start and it's going to be wonderful.*

And they go on and on and on and on some more. They have a nice dinner that night, and it's about 10 o'clock at night. Larry Two's brushing his teeth, getting ready for bed, and who do you think is standing in the shower? Larry One, right?

Larry One says, "Listen, I've been really busy today, and I haven't paid any attention, but I don't remember seeing you at all."

And Larry Two said, "Oh, you didn't, but let me tell you the story." And, he ran through the story, right?

Larry One says, "Hold it, Larry Two. When you were doing construction work for a lousy $10,000 a year, you went to work every day, and you were there on time, and you showed up every single day. And I'm paying you $100,000 a year, and one of your friends comes by, and you don't go to work at all?"

He said, "I need more consideration than that. If you're not going to work like you say you're going to work, then we're going to adjust your pay schedule here, Larry Two. It's going to be adjusted."

Now, Larry Two could look at that two ways. Well, that's being really hard. You bet your life it's being really hard. Larry One cares about Larry Two, and he's not going to let that habit start.

If he lets it start, it's going to happen three weeks from Thursday. He'll be doing it every single day. He'll be starting to slack off because of habits. Lack of discipline starts to creep in.

Everything rocks along fairly well until all of a sudden one day, Larry Two is supposed to talk to 10 people, and he only talks to eight people, and he's heading home, and he said, "Oh, my goodness. Aw, it's just been a terrible day. I tell you though, these eight that I talked to are better than any 20 that I could have talked to. Oh, yeah, these eight are good." He pulls up in the driveway, and who do you think is leaning next to the garage door? You guessed it. Larry One.

Larry One says, "Oh, I've been really busy and everything, and I hadn't talked to you lately, but I only counted eight today."

Larry Two nonchalantly says, "Oh, it was eight, but blah, blah, blah."

"Larry Two, I pay you for 10 a day, not eight a day. If you want to get paid for eight a day, fine. We'll adjust it, but I ain't going pay $100,000 a year for only eight."

Larry Two agrees, "You're right," and he gets in his car, and he pulls out the driveway. The first car he sees that has two people in it, he says, "Pull over," right? He is hungry, and he wants to go home.

See, here's the tendency. The tendency is for Larry Two to say, "Sure, so what it's 9:07, so what? I don't have to be that strict," or "So what if I miss a day and one of my friends comes over?" or, "Alright, I only talked to eight a day. Big deal. I'll make up for it."

The tendency for Larry Two is to lie to himself by saying, "I'm doing okay." Let me tell you this,

You didn't get into direct sales or
any other business for yourself to do okay.

Every single one of you in this room was doing okay before you found Herbalife. That's not why you're here. If you got here to do okay, you're doing entirely too much work. There's a better place to spend your Saturday afternoon than here with us if you want to do okay.

Okay, everybody does okay. There's no big deal about doing okay. They don't write you up in the *LA Times* or *People Magazine* for doing okay. *Okay* is not a big deal. There are no commendations for doing okay. Nothing happens. Your family doesn't look up to you for doing okay. Your wife doesn't go out here and get you special dinners for doing okay. That doesn't happen. You get okay responses for okay effort.

You got into your business because you wanted to do excellent. You got into your business because you wanted to do outstanding.

That's why you got into your business. You wanted to do exceptional things, not *okay*.

It's too hard to be in your business and just do *okay*. You've got to learn to employ yourself. You understand? Your habits will definitely determine your income.

Your Mental Projector

You are the Projectionist.
Learn to Choose What You Feel!

I'm going to draw you a picture here. And I'm not much of an artist, so I'm going to have to explain it. This is the picture that kind of put it all together for me.

I learned this *employ yourself* concept. I had to learn that stuff. Nobody showed me this. Nobody explained procrastination to me like I

We need a drawing here

explained it to you. I had to learn it. You can find out your own stuff. These are things just to stimulate your thinking here, to get you hopefully going the direction that you want to go.

Now, you know how to build an organization, right?

You know who to look for.

We talked a little bit about *controlling your thinking*.

We talked about bad habits and lying to yourself and procrastination.

We showed you how to employ yourself.

Now I'm going to give you a picture here that would bring the whole thing together.

And this picture, what I'm going to draw for you, for this little box, and you need to put this on your notes, this is a projector. And this projector is much like the projector that we show the film presentations on at night. Now, if you're going to have a movie projector here, a movie projector by itself is nothing. You have to have some elements.

One thing that you need, you need a screen, right? If you're going to see it.

You also need some films, don't you? You've got a list of films to choose from.

This is really important to understand. We have a projector, we have a screen, we have films. In between the projector and the film, we have choice, which means we choose the film. Right? We choose what film we put in the projector. If everything's working right, it shows up on the screen.

Now, you invite me over to your house. And, you've got these new films you want me to see.

You invite me over and say, "Oh, I've got these new films. You're not going to believe it."

I'm excited to see what you've got, "I'm coming, I'll be there." I show up and we do the chit chat, we get all down, we get comfortable and talk and everything. And I say, "Okay, I'm ready."

You ask, "What film would you like to see?"

And I say, "I've got to see *American Pie* again."

"Okay, I'll get the film and the projector, I'll get all set up here, and you get the popcorn." (The natural popcorn, of course.) "It's going to be something. My new sound system is in, it's wonderful."

"Alright, I can't wait!"

Got the popcorn, you've got the film loaded. Okay, we let it rip. We chose to see *American Pie.*

Now, lights go out. Projector goes on. Light comes on the screen. The credits start to roll, and instead of *American Pie* it's *Elephant Man.*

I immediately say, "I thought we were going to see *American Pie.*"

You say, "Me too."

"Well, you've got the wrong film in the projector." Right? If *Elephant Man* is showing on this screen, what's in the projector? Projectors aren't known for playing real tricks, you know what I mean? They're pretty conservative, they don't do radical things.

So, do we agree that if *Elephant Man* is showing on the screen that *Elephant Man* is in the projector? No matter what, right? No matter what you think is playing, *Elephant Man* is in the projector, period, over and out. We all buy that story, okay?

Now, we're going to change this just a little bit. We're going to change these films. I'm going to call this film, *Positivity*. We're going to call this film, *Negativity*. We're going to call this one, *Success*. We're going to call this one, *Failure*.

We're going to call this one, *Love*. We're going to call this one, *Hate*.

We're going to call this one, *Happy*. We're going to call this one, *Sad*.

The screen becomes the screen of life. The projector gets changed just a little bit, and we're now going to call this, *The Mind*.

Choice is exactly the same.

Now, a person says, "I have a real positive attitude, but *Negativity* is showing up on the screen." What's in the projector? *Negativity*.

And, another person has *Failure* consistently showing on their screen of life and they say, "It can't be *Failure* because I know I'm thinking successfully?" If *Failure* is showing on their screen, it cannot be coming from *Success*. What's the answer? They've got the *Failure* film in the projector. Remember about lying to yourself? That's what's happening.

The person who has *Success* on the screen, what do they have? *Success* playing in the projector.

Happiness, sadness. If a person's constantly sad, they've got what film is in the projector? *Sad* film. They want to be happy, what do they do? They plug in the *Happy* film.

Now, a person is having a great day with a *Positive* film in the projector, and they have a blowout tire at 4:00 pm on the Harbor Freeway right out here. Now, that's a true test of their attitude. What's going to happen now? Is their film going to change from positive to negative or are they going to keep the same film in the projector regardless of circumstances?

> **Whatever is showing on your screen is because of what is in your projector. When there's adversity is when you find out what you really think and really believe.**

Anybody can look good when things are going well. Well what about adversity? What do you do then? That's when your true colors come out. Whatever is on the screen is in the projector. And not only do you see what's in there, everybody around you sees what's on your screen of life.

Now, when I realized this I said, "You mean to tell me…" (Remember my thing? Only $25,000 a year. It's all I could think. Remember my deal? Construction work, that's all I could think. I could only see past that one little house that I was going to get, that one deal was all I could do.) I became aware, and I put more things into my projector. And I'll tell you, when I first realized this, I went to work on this one in a positive/negative sense.

Positive. Negative. Positive. Negative. I'd be going along there and every two or three minutes, I'd have to change my film. Every two or three minutes I'd be going along there and say, "Oh my goodness, I've had the *Negative* film in for the last two minutes." And I'd just reach down there and plug in the *Positive* film, right?

You think that's okay. You are set. For about two minutes, then I had to switch them back and forth. I still have to do it today. Today, I'll be going along, and I say, "No wonder things have been going bad, I've had the wrong film in the projector for two days. Two days!"

And then, I put the right film in, and I'm alright for two or three weeks. I still have to do this, just like you're going to have to do it. Find out whatever is on the screen because you've got that film in there. Remember, the key factor here is choice. You get to choose the film.

Problem Solving

Learn to Handle Problems Quickly and Efficiently

Success is a habit, unfortunately so is failure. Vince Lombardi said, "Winning is a habit, but so is losing a habit." Vince Lombardi built the Green Bay Packers dynasty (which nobody thought that he could do.) Following a game, Lombardi and the team reviewed the films the next day. He was more upset if they won and played sloppy, than when they lost but played well. Now why would that be? It wasn't about winning or losing; it was about habits and how they played the game.

Vince Lombardi understands habits. You've got to correct these habits; you've got to work on the habits. One of them is problem solving. We have to talk about problems here. Now to talk about problems, I'm going to have to draw you another picture.

It's a walnut, okay. Why do you crack a walnut? To get inside. Why do you want to get inside? Because the goodies are inside.

All the goodies are inside the walnut, right. So, the walnut right here does you no good, but if you crack the nut, you get inside to the goodies, and you get to eat all the goodies. You're entitled to it because you cracked the nut, right?

Problem solving is a lot like walnuts, it is. You have to learn to solve problems. Here's a formula:

Problem solving equals maturity.

Maturity equals personal growth.

Personal growth equals production.

And, you've got to produce.

So, you've got that problem-solving equals maturity, maturity equals personal growth, personal growth equals production, which is your income.

My point to that is don't shy away from problems.

Don't see how many problems you can get away from, see how many problems you can figure out how to solve.

The bigger the problem, the bigger the paycheck, remember that.

If you solve just everyday problems that everybody can solve, then that's called an average problem solver, average income. The only difference between someone making a living and someone making a fortune is they ask for bigger problems to solve.

Mark Hughes asked for a big problem to solve. How to get fine quality, natural herbal products in the market to control people's weight that would be good for them? And, get it at an economical price? And, to develop up an organization to do it? That was a problem that Mark Hughes had 13 months ago, he solved it. It's solved, yes.

Bigger problems, he could have had the same problem, the same intensity with putting in his lawn in the backyard. The only difference is the paycheck. The bigger the problem, the bigger the paycheck.

Let's talk about babies here for a minute, okay. This is going to be interesting. Babies have problems and when a baby has a problem, how do they let you know about it? They cry. You know when a baby's got a problem because they cry. Let's talk about some of the problems that a baby could have. One of them could be that they're hungry, right, if they're hungry they cry. Then you say, "Oh, I should feed him, right?"

Another problem could be sleepy, could be tired right and want to go to sleep. Another one is, they could be wet, need to be changed. Or, there could be another one where they could be stuck.

Those are the basic problems that a baby has, babies don't have problems other than that. Do you agree they have very few problems?

Adults have problems too, an adult that is immature goes about it the same way a baby does, they cry. They cry about the problem, they don't solve the problem, they cry about their problem. They put their problem on somebody else and that equals immaturity. You have got to learn to crack the nut, okay? So, you get the goodies inside.

Now, sometimes you go to all the trouble of cracking this nut and you don't get what you think. You crack that nut and get inside and you discover there's no goodies inside at all, there's a worm in there, right, so you don't get paid for that.

Usually when you have to solve problems with worms in them, it involves people. You've got to remember this, the majority of the problems that you're going to have to solve in your life have very little to do with policies and rules and regulations.

The majority of problems you're going to have to solve are going to be personality problems that have to be dealt with.

Sometimes, you'll get inside one of these walnuts, and there will be a worm in there. That's called a self-inflicted problem. A lot of people have self-inflicted problems. They want you to help them crack the walnut. Why? For one thing they need attention.

You've got to find out what are good walnuts and what are bad walnuts. If you examine a walnut real closely, you can generally tell if there's going to be a worm in there. But sometimes they'll fool you. Sometimes you'll crack it and you'll go all the way through it and then you'll find it there. But when you find a walnut with worms in it, and there's no goodies, there's no growth either. There's no growth for them, and you don't grow from it.

There are no rewards from it, but you have to suffer through it. You have to suffer through it because you're a nice person, that's why you have to do it, okay. There are two types of problems you can't solve.

One of them is an emotional involvement. You can't solve a problem that you have an emotional involvement with. You can't solve that kind of a problem. If you do, you'll come up with the wrong decision if you're emotionally involved in it. If you're emotionally involved, you have got to turn it over to somebody else. Anything you're emotionally involved in, you'll come up with the wrong decision.

The second one that you can't solve is when your hammer isn't big enough. You need more experience to be able to handle the situation, so you have to call on your sponsor or mentor; you have to call on somebody else to solve it. You have to call on someone you have confidence in. A third person perhaps, but your hammer is not large enough to solve that problem, Okay now, in solving problems, here's the thing, write this down:

There's no perfect solution to anything.
You strive for 51% accuracy.

Humanity does not have perfection, period. There are no perfect solutions, but here's what you strive for: You strive for 51% accuracy.

If you're 51% accurate or more on the decisions that you make and the problems that you solve, you are going to win. If you're striving for 100%, you're never going to make it. You want to strive for 51% accuracy, and anything above that you're ahead on.

Now, when someone brings me a problem, knowing in advance that most problems are personalities, here's some steps to it, alright, five steps:

Number One: You've got to gather facts. Under gathering the facts, put enough facts. People say you have to get all the facts. You're never going to get *all* the facts. How do you know you've got them all? What happens after you make the decision and one more fact comes in that you didn't realize?

You're never going to get all the facts, but you want to get enough facts to make a good decision. Enough facts means you've got enough information to see that the picture starts to repeat itself. The picture starts repeating itself from both parties, then you've got enough facts to decide.

Now, here's another picture I'm going to draw you. It's a pancake.

Now here's some things about pancakes that we need to talk about. What does a pancake always have? They don't always have syrup, and they don't always have butter. But, there's two sides to every pancake. Both sides are never the same, one side is always a little browner than the other side, right?

Just like a pancake, there are always two sides to a story. Analogies like this help me in decision making.

There's also a thing called *spotlighting*. Know what spotlighting is? Spotlighting is when whoever brings me the problem first, is usually the person at fault in a personality situation, which most problems are. The first one to bring me the problem is usually in the wrong; it's called spotlighting.

They take the spotlight off of them and throw it onto somebody else. That's what they're trying to do, to get the spotlight off them. They are the problem and they want to draw attention to someone else so that you won't see what the real issue is. They don't want you to see their inadequacies at all.

Number Two: Brainstorm for possible solutions. Possible solutions, every possible solution, there's no perfect solutions remember. Any possible solution, find several, not the correct solution, you're not after the correct solution here, you're after possible solutions.

Number Three: You pick two solutions. You pick what is the fairest for everybody involved, and you also ask yourself something like this: *If I choose this solution this time, would it apply every time?* This is very important here. Because if it doesn't, you're now probably getting involved in what? Personalities. If I choose this solution this time, would it work exactly the same way the next time this same circumstance came up? And if it can't, you need to analyze it.

For example, someone says, somebody stole my prospect, right? Possible solution is you could shoot the guy that stole your prospect, or you could shoot the prospect, right? You just have to brainstorm for solutions.

Here's another part to that. You always have to find somebody that you hold in esteem and you've got to say, how would they handle this situation? How would they do it?

Number Four: You choose the best solution. Choose the best solution, choose it quickly knowing that you will make mistakes. But what's your goal? Your goal is 51% accuracy.

When you choose it, here's what you judge – you judge intent. You've got to judge intent when someone has done something inaccurate, you've got to judge their intent. Was there greed involved? Was there malice involved? That has a great deal to do with it, intent.

They might have done it out of intent, which means greed and malice. They might have done it out of ignorance, which means they didn't know. They honestly didn't know. They might have done it out of stupidity, which means they knew, but they did it anyway. Or they could have done it because they had false facts. So, then you've just got to act accordingly.

Number Five: Act on your decision. Once you've made your decision, you act upon it. You act upon it. You decide, you inform the people involved, knowing in advance that everyone will not agree, but you decide, and you act on it and you never look back on a decision, ever. The bigger the problem, the bigger the paycheck.

When someone brings you a personality problem, you set them down and here's the first three things you say.

First, "Folks before we get started, we have got to understand this, what can I do about yesterday?"

And you know what their answer will be, "Nothing." That's part one.

Second is, "If you're here today to be part of the problem, or you're here today to be part of the solution is going to determine my attitude. If you're here to be part of the solution, we'll talk, if you're here to be part of the problem, it's over. Did you come here today to be part of the problem, or did you come here today to be part of the solution?"

And what will they say? "The solution."

Third, I always say, "I want you to know right now, there's no perfect solution to anything. Now, if you agree to those ground rules, we'll proceed." And, we move forward to a solution.

Now, these concepts will help you in solving problems.

The 7 Diseases of Attitude

Know Them, Be Aware of Them, and Work on Them Diligently!

I want to share a couple of things with you here that I feel strong about. It's called *Diseases of Attitude*. I feel very fortunate in my life that I've been exposed to the type of thinking, the type of training that I'm sharing with you now.

Diseases of attitude are a lot like weeds in a garden. To get a good garden we need several things. If you're going to grow a rose garden, you've got to have several things. You need good seeds, good soil, plenty of water, and a really good hoe to have a good garden, don't you? If you're going to have a beautiful rose garden, that's what it takes.

But in the same area of space, to have weeds, what do you have to do? Nothing. To get weeds, you don't have to do anything at all. Weeds will come up all by themselves. You don't need good ground, you don't need good water, you don't need a good hoe, you don't need anything. Weeds will crop up all by themselves.

You don't have to plant weeds. Weeds are automatic.

Rose gardens you have to plant. Rose gardens you have to tend. Weeds just grow.

See, this applies to all areas of our lives. It's almost like man stands at the garden of his wedding, at the door of his marriage. He looks out there and his marriage is in complete shambles and he says, "I didn't intend it to be this way." And of course not, he didn't intend it to be that way. Nobody intends it to be that way. But it is. And I'll tell you how things get in shambles. It's called neglect.

88

Neglect will do it every single time. One week of neglect can cost a year of repair in your rose garden, can't it? Don't water your rose garden, don't weed it, don't fertilize it for one week in the heat of summer and what's going to happen? It's over for your rose garden.

A person can amble around here for a while and then be lost for a lifetime. You've got to tend your garden. You've got to get out the hoe. And here's some attitudes that we're going to talk about, diseases of attitude.

Number One is INDIFFERENCE.

Indifference is the mild approach to life. Indifference is that shrug of the shoulder. Saying, "Oh, you know I can't get all that worked up about something." That's indifference.

All I can tell you is if you can't get all worked up about something, you need to check your list. If it's not worth getting all worked up over, perhaps it's not worth doing at all, regardless of what it is. Get worked up about what you do.

Swing hot or swing cold, as they say. Even the good Lord said it: I have more respect for the person that does go all the way than the person who's in the half-baked, lukewarm middle here. Strong feelings are what we're after.

Someone's always asking, "What type of people do you like to be around?" My quick answer is always, "Strong-feeling people." I don't care what they feel strongly about. What I want them to do is feel strong about what they feel. It's kind of like back in the real early Christian days. The good Lord needed someone with strong feelings to lead the Christian movement.

Back then it wasn't like it is today. You didn't put 125,000 people in the LA Coliseum to hear Billy Graham on Sunday. Back then, it wasn't good to be a Christian. You didn't go out and publicize the fact and one thing you didn't do was go to the

Coliseum, especially on Sundays. The word was stay away from the Coliseum and the good Lord needed someone to lead the charge. He's looking around for someone and His prime thing that He was looking for was someone with strong feelings.

He looks down there and he sees Saul of Tarsus.

You've got to understand Saul of Tarsus. Saul of Tarsus was probably one of the greatest Romans that ever lived. He was also Jewish and one of the greatest Romans. And he was very intellectual, one of the greatest debaters of the time. Saul of Tarsus was really something. You always knew what Saul was into because whatever Saul was into, he went all the way out for it.

Everybody in the community knew what Saul was thinking. Everybody in the community knew what Saul was doing. He was called, All Out Saul, because he went all out for everything that he did.

Saul only had one problem, he hated Christians. He hated them so much that he killed them. Every place he went, he killed Christians and because he was high up in the community, he had letters of authority to go around and kill Christians every place that he went.

He heard about a new group of Christians starting up in Damascus. You know the story. He got new letters of authority, gathered some men around him and he's smoking it to Damascus to get these new Christians. The story goes that he was breathing threats of slaughter. That means he felt strong about it.

The good Lord looks down there and needs someone with strong feelings and said, "My goodness. Look at that Saul. He really feels strongly. That's my man, right there." A bolt of lightning comes out of the sky and knocks Saul off his horse and blinds him temporarily. (It's a recruiting tool that you and I can't use, but if you're the Lord, you know what I mean? Have at it.)

Long story short, Saul gets converted to Christianity and becomes one of the greatest champions of the early Christian movement; one of the greatest men to ever live; Saul of Tarsus, Paul the Apostle. It was really something.

Strong feelings is what you look for. You've got to put everything you've got into everything that you do. Paul later said, "The things that I once loved, I now hate. The things I once hated, I now love." And that's called strong feelings. See, I don't care what direction a person is going in. I want them to feel strongly about what they feel about.

Put everything you've got into everything you do. That's the formula for real success. That goes from making a fortune to kissing your lady in the morning. *I will promise you that adventure awaits you in both cases.*

Number Two is INDECISION.

Indecision. It's called mental paralysis. Indecision will bring you to your knees. Indecision is when a person is on the fence. They can't quite decide which way to go. Indecision is when a person knows they're crippled with this disease.

The person says, "I know I'm on the fence, but I just don't know what to do." Sometimes you have got to make the decision knowing the 51% accuracy factor and knowing that you have got to get off the fence. It makes no difference what side it's on. It doesn't make any difference if you get off on the wrong side.

What makes a difference is that
you practice the habit of making decisions.

See, a life full of adventure, a life full of success, is a life full of many decisions. Indecision is the greatest thief of opportunity. Indecision is the greatest thief of time, greatest thief of happiness.

You got to learn to decide quicker, you got to learn to decide faster, you got to learn to decide better. Not reckless, not careless, but you've got to decide and move on. Indecision will bring you to your knees.

Number Three is DOUBT.

Doubt is like a plague. The worst doubt that a person can have in their life is self-doubt. It's the worst, to doubt yourself.

A person doubts, "Well, I don't know if I can do all that well." Why would a person entertain that thinking at all? A person doubts if he can make that much money. Remember the projector? If you're going to think about something, why not think about positive things? A person doubts if it'll last that long. Pretty soon people get good at doubting. Pretty soon the person can be a practiced doubter. They get really good at it. And I'll tell you what happens, they end up with an empty cup. An empty cup is what's in it for the doubter.

Turn the coin over, become a believer. Remember that trust is better than doubt. Always. I'm not telling you that you're going to win with that formula every time, but I am going to tell you you're going to win with trust a lot more than you can win with doubt.

Trust is a better deal than doubt.

Number Four is WORRY.

Worry can cause you so many problems:

Worry can cause you health problems.

Worry can cause you social problems.

Worry can cause you personal problems, economical problems, family problems, all sorts ...

Worry can drop you to your knees and reduce you to a beggar overnight.

Worry is a bad habit to get into. You can't be a worrier.

You can't be like the little old lady in Cleveland. She used to say, "My goodness. You know I can't believe this nuclear bomb, the nuclear things going on all over the world. I just can't believe it." She's always worried about a nuclear bomb coming. She said, "If one of those things were to go off here, I'd go all to pieces."

Of course, she would, right? But why go to pieces before the bomb falls? Why do that? To reduce yourself to a beggar overnight?

I used to be a super worrier. I did. Not a super warrior. Super worrier. My family wished I'd have been a super warrior. But I wasn't. Worry. You've got to give it up as a bad deal, worry. You got to treat worry like it's excess baggage.

Substitute worry with positive action. I want you to remember this, the heavy chains of worry, are always forged in idle hours. The heavy chains of worry are always forged in idle hours. Get in action. Take positive action.

Number Five is OVER CAUTION.

Some people are always just cautious. This is called the timid approach to life. Timid approach. Some people always test the water before they take the plunge. They test the water out with their toes before they take the plunge.

Some people wait for better days to come. Better days are never going to be here. You have to take the days as they are and make them into what you want them to be. Better days aren't coming. When has there been a better day? There hasn't been a better day. There are 24-hour segments that we have at our disposal for success/failure, happiness/sadness, positive/negative. There are 24-hour segments every single day; that is what we have.

There's no such thing as better days. There are days. Period.

Take the days how you find them and make them into what you want them to be. I'll tell you one of my biggest cautions always was risk. Risk. I'd say, "Well, what if this happens? What if that happens? And then what if this happens? And then what about that? What if that happens? What about that one, huh?" It used to be my attitude.

There is always risk. Always risk.

People who chronically fail, always look at the risk in the opportunity. People who always succeed, look at the opportunity in the risk. You can't get away without risk.

Nobody's entitled to go through this deal called life without risk. You think you can have success and happiness without risk? It's an impossibility. Nobody gets off without having risk. It's part of our life. Let me tell you. Life is risky. I'll tell you how risky it is, we ain't getting out alive. Try that deal out.

I had someone tell me, "You guys are always talking about opportunity, opportunity, opportunity, here in Herbalife. And what happens if I get going and all of a sudden I start building up a little bit of inventory here, start conducting my business, I'm walking across the street and I get run over by a car, break my arm here, break my leg, and I end up in a hospital, can't work, who's going to take care of my family? Who's going to pay my bills? Herbalife?"

The answer to that question is, "Of course, not."

I'll tell you what I told him, I said, "Listen here, when you're walking across the street, instead of it being a car that hits you, let's have it be a truck. And not only does it break your leg this time, but it breaks your arm, breaks your back, breaks your neck, crushes your skull, you end up in a hospital, complete vegetable for the rest of your life. How about that one?"

He said, "Don't make fun of me."

I said, "I'm not making fun of you. My wreck's better than yours."

You can't design a nice one-legged wreck. Can you? You can't do that. So, if you can't do that, why design any wreck at all? Why look at that side of it? Someone's always looking for safety and security.

Let's say I need safety and security. Well, if you want safety and security, we'll put you in the corner. We'll get you a sheet, we'll get you a blanket, we'll bring you food and water every single day, you'll probably live to be 100 years old, safe and secure in a corner. You say, "Yeah, but what a way to live." That's right. What a way to live. Safe and secure.

Number Six is PESSIMISM.

The pessimist always looks on the dark side. The pessimist always looks at the reason why it can't work, why it won't work. We know the story.

To the pessimist the glass is half empty.

To the optimist the glass is half full.

We know that story. We just got a new place out on the beach. Boy it's nice. You walk outside and you put your feet in the sand, it's just unbelievable. I can't even tell you how good I feel there, and I know I look good, too. That's probably the best part about it. I had a friend over and he said, "My goodness, the taxes must be high here." You step out and put your toes in the sand and he says, "The taxes must be high." Can you believe that?

Got a view that is so beautiful. And, he can't even believe the view, yet he says, "The taxes must be high," and he doesn't even live there. He can't enjoy the sand between his toes and the smell of the ocean because he's concerned about the taxes.

A negative accountant I once worked with kept saying, "What if we go broke? What if we go broke?"

And I kept saying, "What if we get rich?"

See, the pessimist doesn't look for virtue, he looks for faults and once they find the faults, they start to enjoy the faults. The pessimist looks out the window and doesn't see the sunset, he sees the specks. He doesn't see the beautiful painting on the wall, he sees the cracks, how ugly it is. It's ugly. We don't need to be that way. It's not becoming to anybody. I don't care who you are. It's ugly. Get rid of it.

It doesn't take long for pessimism to break your life down to where it's not worth much more than a warm pitcher of spit. Just wanted to get the point across. Didn't want you to forget.

Number Seven is Complaining.

Complaining, crying, griping…spend five minutes complaining and you've wasted five minutes. You can't complain. Who are you to complain to anybody about anything? Where do you get off complaining to somebody about something? Who are you to do that?

Imperfection can't judge imperfection, period. Crying, complaining, griping, it won't work. I'll tell you a story, a story of Old Testament fame, about the children of Israel. It's a good example here.

Through a series of miracles, God got the children of Israel, got them free as slaves and they're heading towards the Promised Land. You know how it goes.

They're going to the Promised Land, got them freed as slaves and they're heading to the Promised Land. They're free now and heading to the Promised Land, not slaves anymore, free, going to the Promised Land.

You know what happened? They started crying, condemning, complaining from day one. They complained about the food, they complained about the weather, they complained about the leadership. They complained about each other.

They complained and they kept complaining and crying and condemning so long until God got it up to here, I guess. And He said, "Trip canceled." They never made it. They died in the wilderness.

Going to the Promised Land and crying and condemning and complaining, they never made it to the Promised Land. That's how serious that one is.

Those are the seven diseases.

You've got to know about them.

You've got to work on them.

You've got to become aware of them.

Five Major Ingredients to Turn Your Life Around

Apply them at the Same Time for Predictable Results

All of us are here today. We came here today to turn our lives in a new direction. We're not here for anything else. You remember that deal about lying to yourself? Tell yourself while you're here today, there are a lot of other places you could be besides spending four hours at the Bonaventure Hotel with us. You could be at any place you wanted to be.

You're here today because you want your life to be turned in a new direction. There are some ingredients that have to take place. There's five major ingredients (I'm going to share them with you here) that go into the day that turns your life around.

These ingredients have to be in a 24-hour period, 24-days per month, 24-months, but there are some ingredients, five major ingredients that goes into turning your life around.

The First Ingredient is DISGUST.

You know what a disgust means? Disgust means you don't like it like it is. Disgust means that you had it up to here. You're not putting up with it anymore. No more will you live with it like this. See, a person could have it with embarrassment of not being able to pay their bills on time. They say, "I have had it, no more."

A person could say I've had it with giving a dollar when they always want me to give more. A person could have had it with a sick feeling, when a man knows that his wife is down at the store shopping and she's looking at beans, two cans of beans, one marked 37 cents, one marked 39 cents and he's sick inside knowing his wife is going to choose the 37 cent can of beans and she doesn't even like the brand. You know why? To save two cents. And the man says, "I'm not living like this anymore. I have had it. No more are you going to see me on my knees in the dust looking for pennies. I'm going to do something about it."

When you see a man could have it with mediocrity. He could have it with not being some kind of winner. He could have it with not having challenge. He could have a lack of excitement, love and caring, but when a person says, "I've had it," I'm telling you, look out. That could be the day.

The Second Ingredient is DECISION.

You have to know what you want. Almost everybody in my life that I've met can tell me what they don't want; but almost no one in my life I've met can tell me what they do want. Most people spend more time planning their three-week vacation every year, than they do planning their future. You've got to find out what you do want, and I'll tell you this about decision. It's not easy. Decision is not easy.

Winston Churchill called it, *The Agony of Decision*. You don't want that agony of decision, that sick nausea feeling. You get that cold sweat pops out on your forehead. You're lying in bed late at night. It's a midnight hour, but you've got to decide. I'll tell you what I've found out in my life, that generally making a decision is the hardest part. That's the hardest part of almost anything I've ever done is the decision. If a person could just wade through the heavy waters of decision, they could climb the mountain almost every single time.

The Third Ingredient is DESIRE.

You have to *want to*. This whole book has been about these five ingredients. You have got to *want to*. You've got to develop your *want to*. I wish someone had desire for sale. I do. I wish that we could package it in little bottles, because if we could package desire and you could take a couple of tablets and they would increase your desire every day – watch the wheels come off!

Here's what I would do. I would tell you to go home and liquidate all your assets and come back and buy every bottle of desire your money will purchase. Buy every bottle of desire because that's where it starts. I'll tell you this about desire – it comes from deep within you. You can't clip out a coupon in the magazine and send for it. It doesn't work that way. It cannot be bestowed upon you by some benevolent magistrate someplace. You have got to develop it.

Your desire can be cultivated. It can be cultivated by a meeting like this today. It can be cultivated by getting involved with a group of people. It can be prayed for. A lot of it comes from books that I've read, people I've met, my family. The only thing I'm sharing with you here is every single day, add more weight to *your want* and ask for it. Search for it.

Fourth ingredient is ACTION.

Decision can turn you in a new direction; it's action that takes you in that new direction. I'm going to give you a word to go with action – *massive*. It's called, *massive action*. Take all-out, massive action. Don't be like the distributor who says, "Okay, I'll pass out a few brochures." He'll always be broke. Don't be like the one who said, "Okay, I'll make a few contacts." Listen, you can guess their bank account. Or, like the girl who says, "All right, I'll try a sales party and see what happens." Listen, that's not the success, that's not how you keep from starving to death.

If you're going to take action, take enough action, massive action so the community won't have pity upon your family. You know, do something that's all-out and massive. Real, sustainable success comes from all-out, massive action.

Fifth Ingredient is RESOLVE.

Resolve simply means, *I'll do it*. Resolve means, *I'll be there.* Resolve means, *You can count on me.* Resolve means this: You pick out your mountain in life, wherever that mountain is, whatever mountain that is, and you say, "I'm going up to the top." And, you do that.

And there's going to be people to tell you, "You can't climb mountains, you don't have any experience."

You say, "I'm going to the top."

Someone else will say, "Come on, choose another mountain, that's too rocky."

You say, "I'm going to the top."

Someone else will say, "Come on, not that one... That's too slippery."

And, you say, "I'm going to the top."

See, there's something about when someone makes that kind of commitment to themselves, there's something about it that does it. You see, I remember the things in my life that I took a wishy-washy way of attitude. I remember when my daughter used to come to me and say, "Listen, Dad. Can we go on a picnic this weekend?"

And my answer would be, "Sure," but nothing would happen. I couldn't understand when she went away, she wasn't happy. Kids are smart, they know. They know the slightest little thing. She knew that if the wind blew that weekend, we weren't going. If someone got a headache, we weren't going.

Now she would come and ask again, and the answer would be either, *yes* or *no*. And she was just as happy with a *no* as she was with a *yes*. Just as happy. Why? Because either way, the result was going to be the same. We were not going to go on a picnic. I had no resolve to do that.

So, you got to practice a little resolve every day. Whatever it is, you're climbing that mountain. You got to have the "do or die" attitude. That is what you've got to have. Someone tells you, "You can't go up it's too rocky, too steep, too slippery,"

You say, "Listen, here, I'm going up. You're either going to see me waving from the top or dead on the side. I'm not coming back."

Now that's called heavy resolve. There's something about the *do or die* attitude. It's almost like if someone has to do it or they'll die. It's almost like time, faith, and circumstance come together, have a hasty conference, and they say, "Listen, John says he's going to do it or die, we might as well let him have it." Resolve moves providence.

You've got to be willing to practice the little resolves, or the big ones will find you hiding in the closet every single time.

You are Enough
Demand the Best of You

What we've been talking about here today, is getting favorable results in our lives. Those favorable results come from right inside here (points to self). That's where they come from. You don't have to have any special talents, any special energy, any special anything. You have got enough of everything you need right now. I want us all to know something. We've been selected for this Herbalife team, we have.

There are always success stories, before and after. And there's going to be a time in the next two, three, five, seven, 10 years (I don't know how long it's going to take), when Herbalife is the finest company of its kind. And we'll be written up in the magazines, and over here is going to be the "before and the after" pictures.

Someone's going to be reading and say, "What a wonderful success story. Look at that. A schoolteacher did that. Look at that. A construction worker did that. A homemaker did that. Look at that, a doctor. Listen, look at them now. Isn't that something? How come I never found out about these opportunities?"

And they might be walking by that hallway right now, this minute, and never find out about Herbalife. Things don't just happen. Things happen just - and you're here today for a reason, and you need to pay attention to that reason. And we've all been selected for it.

I want you to know right now that you've got enough ability right in your entire being to make this thing work for you right this second. You've got enough to make it work. The difference is going to be in the little things that you do. See, I'm a big sports fan. I really like football, too. Let's talk about spring training.

The rookies always check in to camp before the veterans; they have to work there first. You know the difference between the first-year rookie and the 10-year veteran? They both have the fundamentals of the game the same and that's what I'm trying to share with you. You got enough fundamentals right now to make it work.

The difference between the veteran and the rookie is that the veteran becomes the veteran because they do a little bit more, they become a little better every single day, every day. It's done in inches; it's not done in yards. It's done in inches.

That's that little bit of extra excitement that you're going to have to muster up, that little bit of extra attitude control that you're going to have to have, that little bit of extra sincerity, a little bit of extra faith, that little bit of extra fun.

You have to live up to your best.

You have got to demand the best out of you!

If you can't demand the best out of you, then you need to take a real strong look at everything that you're doing. No matter what it is. Joseph Kennedy had a sign on his desk, and when I heard about this, it really helped me out because I was always real tough on myself. Do you know what that signs said? It said, "Once you've done your best, the hell with it." And that's all I'm saying to you today.

> I want you to learn to be strong in your life,
> all areas of your life. I want you to learn to be strong,
> but I also want you to learn to develop your strength
> without being rude. Become strong, but don't become
> rude.

I want you to learn how to win in life, win in
everything,
win the conversation game, win everything,
but learn to win without pressure.

I want you to learn how to be bold,
learn how to be bold without becoming a bully.

I'd like to see you learn how to develop your pride
in everything that you do. Have pride in it - but develop
pride without arrogance. Pride without arrogance.

I'd like for you to learn how to be thoughtful
about all things and everybody, and about yourself.
Learn to become thoughtful without becoming lazy.

I'd also like for you to learn to develop your
humility. Become humble, minus timidity.
Become humble, but don't become timid.

I'd like for you to learn to become kind. Kind to
everything and everybody, especially to yourself. But
develop kindness, without weakness. Become kind,
without becoming weak.

I'd like for you to learn how to become gentle but
become gentle without becoming soft.

I'd like for you to learn how to make new
commitments every single day to your faith, your
family, to your friends, and to your future. I'd like to
see you learn how to be willing to sacrifice the small
things in life, the things that are truly important.

Helen Keller said something once, and it really stuck with me. I'm going to close today with it because I think it kind of says what it means to me. What she said was, "Sometimes the most beautiful things in the world cannot be seen or heard. They can only be felt in the heart."

And that's how I feel about this afternoon and I wish you all good luck. Thank you very much.

ABOUT LARRY THOMPSON

 With a successful 50-year career in the Direct Marketing Industry, Larry Thompson is an innovative executive who transforms products and brands into industry leaders. His formula for success was created from humble beginnings and is the underlying principle from which he has launched many start-up companies and successfully matured them to public offerings. Larry was a distributor and mentor for many direct marketing organizations prior to beginning Herbalife International with Mark Hughes.

Herbalife International embarked on a new market segment with herbal remedies and began selling products from the trunk of their cars. This new market segment became a category creator for the wellness industry. Larry was intricately involved in the first 11 years of the Herbalife, International building and history and directly responsible for some of the decisions which enabled them to sustain their market position now 40 years later.

Larry is a bottom-line executive supported by progressively responsible experience throughout his career. His sales leadership acumen allows him to consistently navigate complex dynamic environments, in the US as well as multi-nationally. Larry is very effective at developing sales strategies and devising effective measures to build and grow organizations. He is skilled at contract negotiation, agreement structuring and operational level agreements to create long term ROI maximization.

As a consultant he provides invaluable experience to startup companies and companies that are matured in their sales strategy to provide energy that's needed to explode sales growth. A dynamic leader in the direct selling and network marketing industry, Larry developed and simplified sales strategies, which companies today still try to emulate.

He is a masterful communicator, effective negotiator, and motivational team builder, known by many as the "Mentor to the Millionaires." Larry is a dynamic trainer and motivational speaker with engagements nationally as well as globally. Over twenty years ago, he developed a wealth building mentoring system, which today is still the most highly sought-after training in direct sales and network marketing; standing the test of time because of its underlying principles.

Printed in Great Britain
by Amazon

43670443R00071